George Bush

Letters From Abroad

Scraps from New Zealand, Australia, and America

George Bush

Letters From Abroad
Scraps from New Zealand, Australia, and America

ISBN/EAN: 9783744695237

Printed in Europe, USA, Canada, Australia, Japan

Cover: Foto ©Andreas Hilbeck / pixelio.de

More available books at **www.hansebooks.com**

LETTERS FROM ABROAD;

OR,

Scraps from New Zealand, Australia, and America.

BY

H. B. T.

PRINTED FOR PRIVATE CIRCULATION.

GLASGOW:
BELL AND BAIN, PRINTERS, 41 MITCHELL STREET.
1884.

PREFACE.

TRAVELLING comfortably has become nearly a science, the grand secret of success being a small quantity of luggage, properly selected. For a trip round the world some little thought is, of course, necessary, but the less impedimenta the greater the real enjoyment. Supposing you start in November (you cannot select a more suitable time), and intend being in London by June, then really very little is needed but cool clothing. This journey to the Antipodes can be made inexpensive, £500, or less, should cover everything, including many pretty presents. Any one wishing to make a closer acquaintance than can be made by books with some of the grandest and most enterprising countries in the world, cannot do much better in the time than follow our route. My reminiscences, or rather letters, are very disjointed, but any friend reading the same must please remember that every line was written, more or less, under disadvantageous circumstances, and I have not bothered to revise them. They are simply letters home. Our experiences cannot be altogether uninteresting. There is one thing certain: I give a simple route, and if that be followed the same result will doubtless be gained, viz., a pleasant, moderately inexpensive, and health-giving trip, full of incident and most instructive, with warm and fine weather, from Malta to Liverpool. I have not re-read—or, perhaps I should say, not re-written—a single letter, and my friends will find first and third persons singularly well mixed. I can safely say my travelling companion was staunch and kind, and everything that a man could desire; and may every other "globe trotter" be fortunate enough to find so good a comrade. My only regret from start to finish has been that those I hold dear could not see for themselves the beautiful and singular sights I have tried to describe. Many of the coach drives in New Zealand were made in great discomfort, the food was plain rather than luxurious, and very early rising was compulsory; but, taken all in all, we had little to complain of.

SKELETON ROUTE.

P. & O. Steamer to Melbourne. Scott's Hotel (for men); Menzies' or Oriental for family. Clubs—Melbourne and Australian.

Union Steamer to Bluff, New Zealand, *via* Hobart and Milford Sound. Rail from Bluff to Invercargill.

Invercargill, Albion, or Prince of Wales—Rail to Kingston (Lake Wakitipu). Steamer to Queenstown and Head of Lake. Back same route to Invercargill.

Rail to Dunedin. Grand Hotel. Fernhill Club.

Rail to Christchurch. Coker's Hotel. Christchurch Club.

Rail from Christchurch to Springfield. Coach to Hokitiki. Return same route to Christchurch.

Rail to Lyttleton. Lyttleton to Napier by Union Steamer. Napier Criterion Hotel and Club. Coach from Napier to Ohinemutu. Lake Hotel. Work Hot Springs and The Terraces, and back to Ohinemutu.

Coach to Hamilton. Rail to Auckland. Star Hotel and Club.

Union Steamer to Sydney. Petty's Hotel. Union Club.

Sydney by A. & S. U. Co.'s Steamer to Brisbane. Queensland Club or Criterion Hotel.

Rail to Warwick; and same route back to Sydney.

Sydney by Pacific Mail Steamer to San Francisco.

Rail to Madera. Coach to Yo-semite Valley; and back to Sacramento.

Rail to Salt Lake City. Metropolitan Hotel.

Rio Grande Railway to Denver. Windsor Hotel.

Denver Rail to Chicago, by Burlington Route. Chicago Palmer House.

Chicago, by Michigan Central, to Niagara Falls. Clifton House Hotel.

Rail and Steamer to Toronto. Queen's Hotel.

Toronto, by Steamer, to Montreal. Windsor Hotel.

Rail, Steamer, and Stage to Saratoga. United States Hotel.

Night Mail to New York. Fifth Avenue, or The Brunswick.

Steamer *Pilgrim* to Boston.
New York, *via* Oregon, to Liverpool.

In writing these Letters I had but one ambition—that of being faithful. If I have been guilty of plagiarism, my memory and not my eyesight must bear the blame. I hate looking back and re-reading words I have written just as the impulse was on me, for nearly all expressions on second reading look weak and inadequate. I can only hope that those who wade through the following pages will retain some few scraps of information likely to reward them for the trouble.

CLIFTON, 1884.

LETTERS FROM ABROAD;

OR,

SCRAPS FROM NEW ZEALAND, AUSTRALIA, AND AMERICA.

LETTER I.

S.S. CARTHAGE,*
22nd November, 1883.

FAREWELL is not a pleasant thing at the best of times, but especially trying when the time must come for 13,000 miles to separate you from those you hold dear. As the tender *Tilbury* steamed away, we could see nothing but a mass of heads and umbrellas. We waved a last farewell, then set to work getting our baggage into the state-room, and many Bristolians would have laughed to see our late High Sheriff struggling with some heavy portmanteau down the narrow companion. As I write the rush and confusion is over, our little space quite neat and ship-shape. The cabin we occupy is said to be one of the best in the ship, but very small, and we can hear the thud of the screw and feel a slight vibration. The *Carthage* is a grand steamer, built by Caird, of

---

* P. and O. steamer, 5,000 tons, 5,000 H.P., 43 feet beam, 430 feet long. Cost £160,000.

Greenock, and specially adapted for hot climates. Even now, although there is a heavy roll on, I am able to write. The saloon at night is beautiful beyond description, lighted by dozens of duplex lamps, with plain white globes, the crimson curtains over the dead-lights give warmth to the scene; palms and other foliage plants give grace, motley humanity adds animation, a bird singing overhead gives an idea of home. As yet I cannot say much about our fellow-passengers, but feel sure we shall easily manage to pick up information and amusement. We have a seat near the Captain, and close to the F—— (friends of the R——). We dined fairly well at six o'clock. A glass of toddy and a quiet smoke finished an exciting day. By this time to-morrow our " home will be on the horizon."

23rd Nov.—During the night hail fell heavily: a N.E. wind made a big roll and brought everybody on deck in greatcoats and thick wraps; few ladies looked really happy, and many men had a "greenery, yellery," over the side look. I am writing in the smoking-room, a stuffy little place, hardly in keeping with so fine a boat. The Lascars act as sailors; they are very inferior to our Jack-tars, but answer the purpose, being cheap and used to hot climates.

24th Nov.—During the night a big sea came over, and, using the carpenter's bench as a battering-ram, forced its way through a companion door, flooding the passages and cabins. Thank goodness no water got over our combing, but many others fared badly. A south-west wind having raised a pretty big sea, the good ship *Carthage* rolls along at ten knots. Every now and then a big slop would tumble over, and away goes crockery, glass, and chairs; really the former must be fearfully and wonderfully made, for it stands no end of knocking about. We passed and sighted a few wind-jammers (*alias* sailing-ships), but saw no steamers. Very cold, clammy, and damp. Even now I can't say much for my fellow-passengers, for the greater number are down below; but the Captain (Hector, R.N.R.), is a man of 50 or perhaps more, medium height, gray hair, with nice manners, eyes bright and gray, with a rather stern look; but I daresay, when we get to know him, he will prove agreeable. The doctor is a perfect gentleman, as far as we can judge by outward appearances; he is about 35 to 38, with rather a military bearing; clean shaven, saving a heavy moustache, broad shoulders, fine figure, and decidedly handsome. Besides this, he has an easy, well-bred manner of speaking, and looks altogether a splendid advertisement for the company whose uniform he wears. The sea is getting up, and I fear a bad night.

Sunday, 25th Nov.—After a somewhat restless night, owing to the clanking and beating of the dead-light chains we both shaved (not an easy thing), went on deck to find a very heavy sea on, and a nasty downpour of close, warm rain. Every now and then she lifted a big slop over the main deck, flooding out many of the second-class cabins. The more one sees of this grand ship the greater the sense of security. Service out of the question, although we have three parsons on board. The nice little lady (A—— know the one I mean) has not yet put in at meals. Most of the passengers are paying debts to Neptune, and the music down our corridor is rather dismal.

Towards evening the wind freshened, and at ten p.m. we were driving at half speed in the teeth of what the Captain called a "fresh gale." The spray was now breaking over her every minute, and scarcely a state-room escaped the water. In more than one the boxes were floating about (at least so the occupants said). L—— and I turned in at 10.30, jammed ourselves into our bunks with wraps and coats, tried for sleep, but at 11.30 the steering gear broke away, the engines were stopped. We were both out and on deck in a moment. There she lay in the trough of the sea literally smothered. The rolling was very heavy, sleep out of the question. The damage was soon repaired, and away we started at half speed. I wedged a box in the doorway to keep out the wet, and placed all shoes, &c., out of reach. After rolling about through a most miserable night, we arose to see the "Bag of Biscuits" in anything but a peaceful mood.

26th Nov.—Very few, indeed, at breakfast, and these nearly all complaining of damp cabins. Sail was set to try and steady her, but the canvas was in ribbons in a few minutes, and the poor Lascars (Lascar, native of Madras) had a hard time of it getting in the torn sails.

Evening found us in fairly steady water, and for the first time since starting we had a really good muster at six o'clock dinner. The breakfast at nine consists of porridge, ham and eggs, chops, Irish stew, curry, rolls, marmalade, &c. The one o'clock luncheon (or tiffin), soup, cold meats, salad, cold tarts, &c. The dinner at six is a good meal of soup, fish, entree, joints, poultry, and the usual pastry, with dessert and coffee.

27th Nov.—The sea went down during the night. We were greeted with a warm and welcome sun, calm sea, and bright faces, and dozens of travellers I had never seen before were up and doing. Everybody on deck putting chairs in order, getting out rugs, and making themselves and each other generally comfortable. What worn, wan faces some of the poor creatures had, and how the terrible trial of sea-sickness was left out of the future torments I can't tell, for really it must be something awful. I have hardly spoken to anybody yet. I do my two miles every day by the pedometer; shall try to keep it up until I get to the Red Sea, and then ——. Please remember as you read this that all has to be written when the *Carthage* is in motion, and the calmest sea produces movement—the screw vibration. The doctor has a capital voice, and gave some really good songs. He seems in great request among the ladies, but some of the husbands look (well, hardly so pleased as the ladies).

28th Nov.—We past old Gib. in the dark, twinkling with hundreds of lights.

Beautiful, sunny day, and delightfully warm. In the far distance the snowy peaks of the Sierra Nevada, and around the deep blue waters of the Mediterranean. Every one on deck, for the most part, dressed in thin clothes; many ladies arrayed in light, gay attire. A quiet day, a calm day, a day for thinking, and inwardly making good resolutions, watching the steamers, ships, and craft, too numerous to mention, passing in silent progress along this great highway. Up to now we have had grand appetites, but I daresay the heat will somewhat alter this. The African coast on the port the whole day. To-morrow we trust to make or rather pass Algiers.

29th Nov.—Another beautiful day; no wind; very cheerful table.

The coast of Africa in view for several hours—the mountains rising tier above tier. Life on board ship, unless we touch land, is of necessity monotonous.

30th Nov.—Last night some dozen or two joined in a dance on deck; altogether it was a pretty sight. The somewhat subdued illuminations of two or three ship's lights, held by dark Hindoos, made the deck a good flirting place. The ladies with bright dresses and flashing jewels (the quantity of jewellery worn all day is hardly to be credited), merry faces, and capital music, formed a very picturesque sight. For my part, I contented myself by turning over the music. During the night a nasty east wind caught the good old *Carthage* dead ahead, washing her face, and dusting her decks in anything but a comfortable manner. Very few at breakfast, old Father Neptune having another good time of it. A poor Seedy boy (stoker, and native of Africa) died on

Sunday from the cold November weather, and was quietly put overboard by his companions, saying, as they did so, some incantation, then reading a portion of the Koran, and finally burning a special kind of incense for the dead, and as the smoke goes upward the soul is supposed to ascend heavenward. Poor fellow! The wind still blowing hard; nobody on deck. The practice for Sunday is *not* going on. Still pegging away, but shall not make Malta until eleven or twelve to-morrow. Nothing sensational up to the present.

LETTER II.

MALTA, 1*st Dec.*—After breakfast everybody appeared intent upon finishing letters, &c. About eleven o'clock the *Carthage* quietly steamed into the Quarantine Harbour of Valetta, the big anchor soon found a bottom, and in a few moments the deck was crowded with eager faces, nearly all dressed in shore clothes. After a brief space, the Doctor came aboard, and as soon as the yellow flag was lowered, a grand rush was made for the gangway. Boat-load after boat-load soon put us on land, amid the shouting of boatmen, the pestering of touts anxious to sell every possible trash, from a Maltese terrier to a globe full of gold fish. These Maltese are a noisy, nasty lot, and the biggest rogues in Europe. Every hotel seemed crowded, to get lunch turned out to be a very difficult affair. Drove round with two or three men to see the Capuchin Church, and once again my nostrils were regaled on pickled monks. Bargained for lace and coins, but could not arrange a price; the Maltese are awful thieves, but on dealing a second time a man is hardly to be had. Smoked cigars, and strolled about the Strada Reale. During the afternoon a nasty fine rain set in; we met groups of fellow-passengers, all looking very wet and miserable. Had a jolly dinner at the Angleterre, and then drove in a body to the Opera, a very fine house, built of stone, cool and comfortable. The Company, playing "La Favorita," was anything but a good one, so at the end of the second act we started to gather up our purchases—two large baskets of oranges, two hats, cigars, cigarettes, prickley pears, and no end of beautiful roses (the latter my only bargain). We had a row with the cabman, who narrowly escaped being pitched into the water. The rain was now coming down in torrents, our party all glad to get into the smoking-room of the good old ship. Coaling went on all night; at six this morning we steamed away for Port Said, hoping to get there about Wednesday, ten o'clock. For the sum of one shilling, I yesterday bought *six large* bunches of beautiful roses. Population of Malta 160,000, of Valetta 18,000, or, perhaps, 20,000. The Valetta market is a curious mixture of beauty and the beast. Flowers in every form and colour, fruit of all kinds, grapes, new figs, pomegranates, prickley pears, &c., vegetables, and beautiful dairy produce, all exposed for sale in filthy dens, each stall presided over by some dirty Maltese; an abominable stench pervades the whole place—beggars, *ad lib.*

2nd Dec.—Rain all gone, warm beautiful sunshine. Service in Saloon; a Church of England clergyman gave us a small thin sermon in a small thin voice, but he looked nice and clean in his gown and Oxford hood—so enough. The singing went off fairly well. Lots of people bought birds yesterday, and the place is quite gay with song. Being Sunday, we have red velvet table-covers, and what, with globes of gold fish, flowers of all sorts, the Saloon is perfect. We landed two or three passengers at Malta, replacing them by others. Shall try and send a line from Suez, or, perhaps, Port Said.

3rd Dec.—Another hot glorious day. Up very early; had a jolly cold salt bath. Got up a Calcutta selling sweep, the total sum collected and knocked down to auction being £20. L—— and I made a calculation, and thought 317 or 319 would be about the winning number, so L—— bought 317 and I 319; we agreed to divide. 317 won, and I received £6 13s. for my share of first prize. After that the passengers met together to select a committee of seven, four men and three ladies, to get up dances, sports, sweeps, music, acting, &c.; how on earth I got 27 votes, is a mystery. Thank goodness the 27 votes left me one vote out of the committee, for I know you cannot go through a voyage like this, without falling foul of somebody, if in any prominent position. Tiffin over, 15 passengers were selected to pull against 15 ship's crew, and after a very few seconds, we, the passengers, pulled them over the line. The next pull was the fossils (over 30), against the boys (under 30). This was a grand pull, and lasted for a long time, and we were winning well, when Dr. D—— got his hand temporarily paralysed, and gave up, so we lost; we are going to try again. Music, singing, and yarns, finished a very pleasant day. The sunset was singularly curious and beautiful, the sky apple green and carmine, with smoke, coloured clouds floating over an apparently *blood-red* sea.

4th Dec.—The heavenly tub, a long walk on deck before breakfast, visiting the cow with the big head, the grouse, pig, sheep, ducks, &c., and speculating with chums as to what the Committee are going to provide for us. For my part, I fancy I see breakers ahead—the parsons and the women are at it, and bitterness, I fear, will result; no meanness at present; but one or two of the ladies are showing venom, what for, goodness only knows. Up to now I have only spoken to one lady (a Mrs. B——), with such a splendid boy; but this afternoon I had one or two invitations to kettle-drum. I declined all, but, mark my words! to-day is the first of a new era. We have one man on board who by common consent is called *The Ass*, and no wonder, for some of his questions are *very* "assinine." Do you think we are doing 30 knots? Is'nt it the sun making the waves? and so on. One of the grouse died to-day, so now there remains only the cock and hen. The refrigerator is hard at work; all meat is more or less tough. Athletic sports came off again this afternoon, most of the men in silk shirts, scarlet scarfs round the waists, white straws, &c., and light or white trousers. The three-legged race created a lot of fun. The fossils again had a tug-of-war with the boys, exactly the same teams as yesterday; the excitement was immense, and we were winning, in fact had pulled them to within one inch of the line, *i.e.*—three yards, (indeed the umpire said the first man touched), but the ladies said no, and Dr. D—— again gave up, and we again lost after a terrible struggle. When I tell you there were more than four pairs of india-rubber soles literally wrenched off with the pressure, you will easily understand what a tug it was. All our hands were swollen. L—— says it was a curious sight to see the Ladies, Hindoos, Lascars, Ship's Company grouped round, all in fits of excitement, clapping and shouting. Many of us had to lie down after. Nearly all the men bought scarlet scarfs at Malta, using them instead of braces; the effect is striking. No gambling on board except the sweep; it is a curious sight to see one or two ladies bidding for numbers under the wing of some gentleman. I have to write in the saloon, with music, singing, and chatting, so please correct any error before you pass this letter on beyond the family. We are all anxious to see the Canal, for such a gigantic work must be interesting. In the selling sweep to-day, I fixed on 315, and bought it for a song (7s. 6d.); L—— did not go halves, and I won this time £8 10s., being the net amount, after deducting 10 per cent., for the Seaman's home. I daresay I shall lose that and more before I get to Sydney. I feel tired, stiff, and sore, after yesterday's pulling—so adieu.

This ship is only driven to do about 300 a-day; she could do more, but the Company won't have it. Washing is a great consideration, and none like to have any done at Columbo, for frequently the passengers contract the "doby itch," from washing done there, so economy is the order of the day. Pitching the 16 lb. bag of sand was heavy work, the longest being 32 feet with one step forward—won by V——, the cricketer.

LETTER III.

6th Dec.—The *Carthage* arrived at Port Said at 6.30. Nearly all the passengers on deck long before breakfast, watching the dark-skinned Egyptians and still more dusky negroes hurrying coal down the hold by means of small baskets. Port Said itself is a mushroom town, brought into existence by the formation of the Canal, oriental and uninviting, swarming with beggars, cadgers, flies, with a fair sprinkling of passengers from the numerous ships going through this narrow highway to the East. This grand work was commenced in 1859, and completed in ten years. The cost was £18,250,000, 100 English miles in length, 66 being actual canal and 22 running through the three lakes—Timsah, Great and Small Bitter Lakes. The width is generally about 325 feet. In one part it is only 72 feet wide. Stations and sidings are situated at various places to allow large vessels to pass each other. The level of the Mediterranean and the Red Seas is nearly the same, thus there is very little current; the little there is flows north from the Red Sea. The rate of speed for steamers is between five and six miles an hour, and the total time being generally twenty to twenty-four hours. From England (Start Point) to Point de Galle (Ceylon) *via* Canal, is 6,515 miles, *via* Cape of Good Hope, 11,650—difference in favour of Canal, 5,135. The above details will give you some outline of the Canal itself, but no words of mine can convey any idea of the dreary sandy plains, with nothing whatever to break their monotony save the long-legged ibis, or perhaps a flight of wild duck. Clay swamps, with a few stunted rushes, are the only uneven things in this bare, parched land. We now and then pass the native dahabieh, a species of boat with a huge lateen sail. A mirage came over the desert this afternoon, we thought we could distinctly see the sea and the waves curling on the shore; but, of course, it was only an illusion. The atmosphere is very clear and cool—in fact, cold. At the present moment we have passed four large steamers, and only two hours in the Canal, and I believe we have four big steamers ahead of us. We paid £1,000 to clear the *Carthage* through the Canal.

DISTANCES.

London to Gibraltar,	. .	. 1,299	miles.
,, Malta, .	. .	. 2,280	,,
,, Port Said,	. .	. 3,215	,,
,, Colombo,	. .	. 6,515	,,
,, Melbourne, .		. 11,185	,,
,, Sydney,	. .	. 12,145	,,

We are just now passing the *Merzapore*, a fine P. and O. steamer. We wave a passing salute. On again, one homeward bound, the other to the antipodes. To-night we have a grand *programme* dance. The hurricane deck is canvased in, decorated with flags, bunting, &c. We have issued invitations to all the passengers of the *Ancona*, another P. and O. boat just ahead of us. About forty or fifty have accepted. At 8.30 the ball commenced. It was really a very gay affair. We had the coloured lights of the ship arranged in two rows up and down our long ball-room. Being in the Canal, and therefore motionless, we were able to dance in comfort. The ladies were dressed in every imaginable costume, some of our guests in low dresses. Nearly all danced fairly well, but after a time it became very hot. A capital supper, a jolly cheer as our guests departed in the steamer's launch, and then a quiet smoke; a big drink of iced soda and B., and then good-night.

To-day I saw growing for the first time in the open air Pointceltia pulcherima in large trees in full bloom, the scarlet very striking.

7th Dec.—Very chilly indeed on deck; a cold wind. Put on my greatcoat, so you can easily imagine the change from the warm weather of the last few days. Going across one of the lakes a storm came on; the Captain became fearful about our going aground; the waves came over the launch, she was left behind for hours with her fires out, and nearly helpless. She is now alongside, and we hope to use her this evening for a return ball on board the *Ancona*. The return ball did not come off, as the distance at sundown (when *all* traffic ceases) from the *Ancona* was over three miles. The blood-orange of commerce is simply the ordinary orange grafted on the pomegranate.

SUEZ.

We anchored in Suez Bay to wait for the P. and O. steamer, *Lombardy*, with the Brindisi mails. Most of the passengers made up their minds to go ashore. Soon the bay on the gangway side of the *Carthage* was crowded with useful-looking boats of the felucca type. Some few passengers were seized bodily and carried off to boats against their will by lusty ruffians of boatmen. One of these abductions occasioned a regular fight between two powerful men, and I shall never forget the slapping, *biting*, wriggling, and frantic grasps of the throat made by these muscular brutes. The first scene of operations was confined to the large step or platform at the bottom of the gangway, whence they were removed with great trouble; but the final battle took place in the bottom of our boat. The two men looked like one mass of wriggling humanity. We soon got Abdallah's opponent over the side, and then, sail being set, we shortly found ourselves at the landing-stage. Another scuffle: donkeys mounted, and a curious cavalcade we looked streaming in single file from the port along the narrow strip of land to Suez proper. One or two riders had a somersault, but all spills were, in my opinion, the fault of the riders, for Mrs. Langtry, The Bishop of Oxford, John Bright, The Grand Old Man, Mrs. C. West, Rachel, Sims Reeves, the Masher, were jolly-like donkeys. My animal rejoiced in the name of Lady Godiva; she had very long hair and very little tail, very little girth and rather short reins, but nevertheless was equal to the two-mile ride, and covered the ground in splendid style.

Fare for boat to shore, each person, . . 1s.
Fare for donkey to Suez, ... 1s.

Suez is, or rather should be, the most healthy town in the world; no extremes of heat or cold; just enough rain to render it cool and fertile, but the sanitary arrangements are simply *awful;* hence it is a hot-bed of every infectious disease known. Less than two months ago the cholera raged here, and at all corners of the streets you can even now see the fumigating ovens. The place is without exception the vilest hole I have ever seen, insect life in veritable clouds. The streets are the original soil simply hardened by the daily treading of 13,000 bare feet. The Suez native bazaar is undoubtedly the most filthy quarter of a mile I have ever walked through; covered with rotten canvas to protect the stall-keepers from the sun. Such stall-keepers! dirty copper-coloured Egyptians, clad in soiled white flowing garments, red-turbaned, and barefooted. Crowds of nearly naked children, most of them with eyes more or less weak, in which they allow the flies to pitch and *remain;* innumerable dogs fighting and tearing the garbage under the stalls, and to that add one *big smell* more than enough to overpower the odour of five good strong cigars, and Suez in a mild form stands before you. Everything is novel and nasty. I was very glad to get into the boat, and sail quietly back to the steamer. As the sun went down the sky became one rich sheet of orange. Abdallah, our boatman, then washed his feet, hands, face. Standing in the bows, facing Mecca, he recited in a clear, soft voice his evening prayer, calling upon Allah, bowing at the same time with deep devotion. Fourteen fresh passengers joined us at Suez, mostly old Australians. Now nearly every seat and berth are occupied.

8th Dec.—As I am writing on deck, we are leaving the Gulf of Suez, surrounded with its strikingly serrated but intensely arid hills, and in a few moments the Red Sea will be entered. Everything quiet and warm. The native barber operated on my head to-day, and cut the hair in a perfect line à la bâsin. The saffron hue of the eastern sky is very peculiar, and lends a lurid look to every thing and person. I believe the Red Sea takes its name from the

Pink Hills on the Egyptian side. I expected to see all the ships' officers attired in the smart white uniform of the P. and O. service, but the Captain was the only one so dressed to-day; doubtless, to-morrow will bring out this suitable costume.

Sunday, the 9th Dec.—At 6.30 the cry of a "Man overboard," and the sudden reversing of the engines brought L——, myself, and dozens of passengers on deck. In fact, we were on deck in a moment. Although only a couple of minutes could have elapsed, the poor fellow was not to be seen with the naked eye. As he went over, two life-buoys were sent after, and as the stately ship slowly backed, we heard the good news from the bridge that the Lascar was safe on the top of both. Soon we could see him waving his hand, his red turban showing bright on the waves. A boat was lowered, and in nineteen minutes he was alongside. I can assure you it was a fine thing to hear the hearty cheer go through the ship as the dark-skinned sailor stepped aboard; we were all afraid of sharks, of which the Red Sea is full. Very warm; all dressed in white or light clothes, the stewards with blue jackets, white shirts, and white trousers, the officers white flannels, and the passengers in every kind of body-furniture, from black frock coats to white silk suits. The best for warm weather and general use is a *very light drab* serge suit and two pair trousers of the same material instead of one. White suits are *nice looking*, but not really *necessary*. The less luggage one has the better. I have about the least on board, but *mine* is far too much. A cheap pith helmet is useful, if bought at Port Said, and then flung away. The smash has come; the whole ship is more or less split up into sets. About a dozen of us, L—— and self included, simply say "How do you do?" to the ladies, but nothing more. The night of the ball two ladies went to bed in a pet because they could not get partners. Thank goodness, the men are all right; and we have no end of pleasant chats in the smoking-room. The ladies are regular cats, and openly say all manner of evil of each other. The husbands have been trying to do what they can, but to very little purpose. Women that I myself have seen gushing over each other less than a week ago now pass staring one another out of countenance. It is most amusing to watch this little game. Of course there are men who might be more pleasant, but, as a rule, in this ship they are all right. The man who is disliked on board ship is the one who insists on having a certain arrangement of his deck-chair without consulting the wishes of his neighbour, or the one who stays in the bath-room twenty minutes, while he knows that ten "pyjamahed and betowelled" unfortunates are standing in a more or less blasphemous state outside in the draughty passage. We used the punkahs to-day for the first time, and found them nice, but not quite necessary. Service as usual, but the parsons having also split up, the affair has fallen out of B——'s hand (an Englishman), and now managed by a long-boned Scot. Afternoon tea is a great thing. You can sit at a table and *literally* hear one set cutting up another. Names and details could afford no real interest to you, so avoid giving them. Heat in cabin very great—I think about 85° at 10.30 P.M. The punkahs make the saloon very cool. They are 2-in. poles, 20 feet in length, with heavy damask hanging 18 inches down, and pulled gently but swiftly by Hindoos in clean white robes and red turbans. We have 15 punkahs in the saloon, and *want* them now.

Monday, 20th Dec.—Some of you may like to know the meaning of the ship's bells, so I will give them under:—

Bells for *fully*-officered steamer—

1 bell,	$\frac{1}{2}$ o'clock A.M.		5 bells,	$6\frac{1}{2}$ o'clock A.M.		
2 bells,	1	,, ,,	6 ,,	7	,,	,,
3 ,,	$1\frac{1}{2}$	,, ,,	7 ,,	$7\frac{1}{2}$	,,	,,
4 ,,	2	,, ,,	8 ,,	8	,,	,,
5 ,,	$2\frac{1}{2}$	,, ,,	1 ,,	$8\frac{1}{2}$	,,	,,
6 ,,	3	,, ,,	2 ,,	9	,,	,,
7 ,,	$3\frac{1}{2}$	,, ,,	3 ,,	$9\frac{1}{2}$	,,	,,
8 ,,	4	,, ,,	4 ,,	10	,,	,,
1 ,,	$4\frac{1}{2}$	,, ,,	5 ,,	$10\frac{1}{2}$	,,	,,
2 ,,	5	,, ,,	6 ,,	11	,,	,,
3 ,,	$5\frac{1}{2}$	,, ,,	7 ,,	$11\frac{1}{2}$	,,	,,
4 ,,	6	,, ,,	8 ,,	12 noon.		

It is next to impossible to give you any idea of this truly beautiful day—a very gentle breeze moving softly under the double awning, renders the heat powerless, and gives a balmy warmth to the body. Sea perfectly calm, without a ripple or motion of any kind. My costume consists of a white coat, white trousers, white silk shirts, and nothing else. The sets are more marked than ever. I have, as I said before, joined *no set*, but I take my afternoon tea with Mrs. B—— and Mrs. F—— (the daughter of Sir H—— R——), both exceedingly quiet nice people; they don't expect you to be always dangling after them. If a man regularly joins a set of matrons and young people on board a ship, I will not say that he is to be always hanging about them, and generally making himself agreeable, but I will say this, that it is expected that he will not make himself agreeable to any other set—in fact, if he shows a touch of disregard all the better. Lemon squash has taken the place of evening grog; I am thankful to say a more sober lot of people I have rarely come across. I intend sleeping on deck to-night, for it gives promise of great heat. I think I may have told you that sometimes a number of emigrants die from "sun-heat" going down the Red Sea, and in June and July (I believe) the government will not allow them to be forwarded. We did sleep on the "main hatch," quite open to the sky and the faint evening breeze, but even with a simple sheet, we were all in a complete bath of perspiration. I slept on until 5.15, when the deck-hose, *by accident*, of course, landed its contents on my head. No more sleep, as you may imagine, for bed, pillows, and self were drenched. It was a curious sight to lie on one's back and see the bright silver moon shining between the spars and the rigging, but my curiosity being satisfied, I shall return to my berth for the future, and brave the heat rather than risk such a cold surprise. We were entertained with a very fair concert for an hour and a-half, but it lacked "go." The sunset was a dusky orange without a cloud.

11th Dec.—About 85° in the shade, but altogether a beautiful day. Passed in the night the straits of Babel-Mandeb (Gate of Lamentations), and in the distance Aden soon came in view.

12th Dec.—L—— and I kept our state-room, but three other men took our places on the main hatch; two set to work, and made the third an apple-pie bed, and of course as C—— (the third man) came down the gangway, they pretended to be asleep, he having gone through his devotions, prepared to get into bed, and discovering its condition, immediately turned the others head over heels, but I cannot portray the bolster fight that took place between these three men. Everything was in ribbons in a few minutes; the audience up above added to the row, by pitching down mats, rope, water, brooms, &c.—how they ever got cool and settled down, remains a mystery. I was awakened by a slap of water through the port, and was very soon enjoying a jolly cold bath, for sleep, after everything is wet, being quite out of the question. Spent afternoon in chatting and reading. The walk after dinner was exquisite—clear sky, soft breeze, dim light from the moon.

13th Dec.—With the same steady head-wind, life has become rather wearisome; bull-board, quoits, cricket, smoking, reading and sleeping form the staple products of a ship's amusements. *No one cares to write;* hence the least pretence to a readable diary becomes next to impossible—but, as I said at starting, I am only writing for those who will take some little interest from its personality. We are all looking forward to seeing Ceylon, and hope to be there for two or three days. A trip to Kandy will be our aim, for the railway ride is one of the most sensational in the world. We have a very perfect machine on board for making ice, and used also for general purposes of refrigeration. We have ices at tiffin, good in quality and quantity. The Doctor has two or three cases of illness, but we all sincerely trust they may not terminate fatally. One young lady (a Miss W——), suffering from great debility and a weakened spine, on her way to Melbourne, to be married; the ceremony should take place two days after her arrival. This I fancy cannot be. She holds a very small levee every afternoon; I generally read and chat to her for an hour or so. My cold still sticks about me, in fact, the immense wind-sails create a draught all over the ship, and dozens have colds in the head—very unpleasant, the colds I mean, about 87° in the shade. I fancy before night we shall run into weather; the motion has suddenly become quite perceptible, and we are passing the celebrated Garde da Fui, noted for the number of shipwrecks—more than a dozen in the last year or so. The current has a set toward the shore—a bare sandy coast, with rocky back-ground. As I am writing a nasty flop has found its way into the saloon, so my words are unfortunately coming true.

Afternoon tea with Mrs. B——, the Captain, and Mrs. F——. The Captain never comes past this coast, except by day; the passage is considered very dangerous. I am invited to a private dinner party this evening, but rather fear the sea will deprive the table of one at least of its number. Very jolly little dinner party—three ladies and three men; the steamer was very good during the meal, but shortly after a north-east monsoon commenced, and in less than an hour no ladies and very few men remained on deck. On my way to my state-room I passed lots of suspicious looking cans, and I very much fear old Neptune is having a good time of it.

14th Dec.—During the night the monsoon gave the *Carthage* a bad dusting; every port closed, a great many ill all night, one or two ladies fainting from sickness and heat, only a *very* few at breakfast. A dead, hard, head-wind, the waves constantly breaking over her bows, very slow progress, and, although I liked the breeze, there was a pretty general show of discomfort. Have I mentioned the thrush? We have a beauty on board, in full song. The remaining grouse are still alive. Have now returned from deck *wet through*, a flop pitched clean over me, so good-bye for to-day. This wretched monsoon will continue all the way to Colombo, may be not quite so heavy—the monsoon is the trade-wind of the tropics. Fancy, I have been on board three weeks! No merry parties at afternoon tea to-day; everybody with a yellow face and quick movement, as they vanish through the saloon to seek the quiet and repose afforded by solitude. Curtain drawn here.

15th Dec.—Confound the monsoon! A dead head-wind, only doing 250 miles; nearly all bad. The ports all closed, and our state-rooms are simply stuffy beyond endurance; the heat *out* of the wind is very great, the good ship sticks hard at it, sending the spray rainbow-tinted all over her bows. We pass through thousands of flying fish, many of these beautiful creatures, making flights from 30 to 70 yards. One old lady last night got into no end of a row, for curling her wig with irons heated from a naked spirit lamp, all lamps save those supplied by the ship's officers being very properly out of order. The Captain told me that he had been in seven ships when on fire, and no less than five fires were caused by ladies. It is nearly impossible to write, for the *Carthage* is pitching very heavily, the waves in Sinbad's sea are anything but tiny. Six ladies fainted last night with the stifling cabin heat; I feel awfully sorry for them, for sickness in a close little chamber must be *very bad*. The *Carthage* is a grand ship.

Sunday, 16th Dec.—The night has been quiet, and the sea having gone down, nothing remains but a long roll. Service but poorly attended. We all of us found the 20 minutes' sermon too much of a good thing. In coming out of the music-room this morning I tried to avoid a lady's dress, and in doing so struck my head against the doorway heavily; but it's nothing now, a quiet rest having put me all right. A number of seedy boys are very bad, the great heat in the engine-room having knocked them up. The doctor has a lot to do, no end of people feeling the heat. Last night I simply lay still and uncovered in my berth, and even then I was literally melted. Since leaving Malta I have been most careful in living. 7.30.—Bath, at nine breakfast—one cup tea, bacon, eggs, chop, toast, and marmalade. *Absolutely nothing* between meals, no matter what the temptation. Tiffin—soup, cold meat, pickles, and two glasses of claret. Cup of tea at four. Dinner and two glasses of claret at six. At 9.30 lemon or lime squash, one cigarette, one cigar, and one pipe being now more than my average. My hands and face are very brown, especially in contrast to my white dress.

17th Dec. (Monday).—To-day, just after breakfast, a white squall came down upon us. The sea at 9.45 was smooth as glass, at ten the whole surface of the ocean was one sheet of white foam. The rush to get the sails, wind-sails, awnings in, was immediate. The howling of the squall, as it struck the ship and tore through the rigging, was a new experience; the sheets of rain, the weird cries of the Hindoos, the rush of passengers to get out of the huge drops of rain, the flying spray—in short, the "nautical stampede" was sudden, unusual, and picturesque. 10.30.—The storm was over, the sea calm, the sun smiling, and the white squall a thing of the past.

18th Dec.—Nearing the Maldives. Palm trees showing indistinct in the early morning. All the islands we passed are only two or three feet above the level of the sea, and the cocoa-nut palms appear to be growing out of the water. Of course, all these islands are of coral formation, inhabited by a race of Hindoos. Sword-fish abound here, some 18 feet in length. Everybody is unpacking, packing, hair-cutting, hair-washing, and very generally preparing for a run ashore. The heat at Colombo is generally excessive, and nine hours in a railway carriage may hardly be thought a treat, but from what I hear the sensation railway to Kandy is unique. I think to-day, for the first time, the cold I started with has left me. The invalids are better. Those who have been paying tribute to Neptune are on deck, and the Great Hotel goes on. If you take the map you will see that we are nearing the equator. We fancy we shall be crossing about Christmas Day; at all events I shall calculate *back*, and at 2.30 I shall do a solitary drink to "absent friends" at home.

19th Dec.—Blowing half a gale; the confounded N.E. monsoon still hard at it. I very much fear that landing at Colombo to-night will be next to impossible. The catamarans, or surf-boats, are dangerous in anything like a rough sea. The rising and falling of the N.E. monsoon is rapid, but the wind always from same quarter. At Colombo the Great Hotel will take in coal, water, fruit, sheep, oxen, eggs, &c., and then resume her voyage.

There is something delightfully pleasant in the voluptuous languor which the soft air of a calm evening in this southern sea occasions, and I fully appreciate lying back in my chair quietly smoking and watching the gorgeous sunset. I shall never forget the impression made by last evening. The sun had just gone down, leaving the sky dyed with the richest tints of carmine, shaded with deep, deep orange, gradually fading away in pale drab, when from the opposite quarter the moon moved slowly upward as bright as silver. The moon at the full in these tropical regions is a glorious sight. We have seen the "Southern Cross," but, as far as we can make out, this constellation is a fraud. In haste for post.

LETTER IV.

21st Dec.—DEAR ALL,—I suppose I must give you some idea of our short visit to Ceylon. Any traveller's book would certainly be more accurate, readable, and probably less expensive, for, by-the-bye, the posting of the last batch of this confounded old diary cost 6s., and I have serious thoughts in the future of giving page so and so of known authors. We went ashore after dinner in a boat pulled by lusty, dusky, noisy, cocoa-nut oil-smelling natives, and soon found ourselves located in the Oriental Hotel, a huge caravansary with a decidedly British twang about everything—the large verandah crowded with the smart, well-set English officer, brawny colonials, bronzed planters, and our charming countrywomen. White costumes for men prevailed, but here and there a dash of colour made the grouping attractive. We retired early, and if my bedroom be a fair specimen, the chance visitor has little to complain of; very lofty and open to the tiled roof, where the green lizard larks about at will, the same pretty creature A—— and I saw together in Italy. The open window has a small balcony, a very convenient perch for the crow; and I can safely say the Cingalese crow is the most impudent beggar in the world (excepting, perhaps, the Christiania sparrow). They fly in everywhere. This morning my next-door neighbour had his toast quietly removed by a sleek and well-to-do gray-headed old fellow while he was shaving. I lay upon the hardest mattress I have ever used, and, adopting the daily dress of the Cingalee, I let my mosquito curtains down and enjoyed the first night ashore. Up at five, and on the platform at 6.45. The line to Kandy is Government property. The Governor himself (Sir Arthur Gordon) and Mr. Plimsoll, of rotten-ship fame, were fellow-passengers during a great portion of the distance. For the first 40 miles the track lies through a flat marshy country, suggestive of fever, ague, &c., but rich in bright green paddy fields (young rice), skirted with batches of cocoa palms and large-leaved forest trees. Behind these clumps the natives build their village of mud huts, all with overhanging roofs. The tawny river Kalingganga moves swiftly to the sea, making Ceylon one of the most productive countries in the world—rich in vegetation, and abounding with precious stones; no bare spot of earth to be seen, the very mountains are covered to the summit. Passed stations, with barefooted native porters, the platforms crowded with brown-skinned children anxious to sell bananas, pines, cocoa-nuts, and dozens of fruits I have never seen before, modestly attired in the brilliantly-coloured handkerchiefs of modern civilisation. Occasionally the saffron toga of the Buddhist priests stood out conspicuous. Soon we commenced the gradual ascent through the mountains, but it is quite out of the question for my pen to even feebly convey to you the brilliant colour and immense variety of tropical flowers expanding to the morning sun. Rain had fallen during the night; every leaf and flower looked bright and fresh. A steamy mist almost insensibly intensified the beauty of extravagant nature. Try and picture to yourselves grove after grove of slender cocoa-nut palms crowned with feathery leaves, and rich in bunches of dark-green nuts, each grove of palms interspersed with huge glossy-leaved trees—names unknown to me. Many of these trees are covered with the tangled orange-flowered lantana ; the alamanda, with its deep yellow bloom twining in contrast to the lilac beaugain-villea, large blue convolvulus creeping everywhere. This repeated in every variety of form will give you some slight idea of our beautiful journey. Close to the line you might easily distinguish large numbers of pine-apples, shaded from dark-green to golden-red. Passed thousands of plantains, strings of green bananas hanging from under their huge flat leaves. Hurrying onwards by small lakes covered with water-lilies in full bloom, striking in variety, each little lake fringed with the fancy-spotted caladium. Here and there a native fishing. Onward past every variety of glossy croton, the scarlet passion flower, intense in colour, hanging in rich festoons. The melon growing at will over some friendly tree or native hut, the pink petalled claradendron trailing over its nearest neighbour, ferns and flowers pushing out from every crevice, the crimson Hibiscus, not content with its single variety, must out-Herod Herod, and charm the eye in every direction with its deep double cluster. Onward and gradually pressing upward by the power of two engines, winding round and round the mountain side, through tunnels heavy with moisture, past coffee plantations, now giving place to the tea shrub or cocoa plant, for I am sorry to say that in Ceylon the coffee plant has failed for years, and many a man, considered to be rich ten years ago, is now poor and nearly hopeless, although still hanging on to property that has depreciated fully 75 per cent. Ceylon is a hot-bed for snakes of many kinds. Amongst the most inviting I fancy the cobra, tickpolonga, rat-snake, anacrite; after the bite of this last, the blood is forced in dying agony through the pores; and to give some idea of the number, I will mention the plan generally carried out in a bungalow, viz., to balance large nails on the iron open work of the verandah round the bedrooms, so that the nail may fall as noisily as possible on the stone beneath, and thus give notice to the native of the presence of these nasty brutes. Butterflies are numerous, but, as far as I can judge, feathered life is rather scarce. I was fortunate enough to see a jungle crow—black body with red wings.

Sensation Rock is about the highest point of this grand engineering work, and the line is simply cut into the side of the solid cliff. As you look out of the carriage window you see nothing but the bright green paddy fields hundreds of feet below, the edge of the cliff being less than two feet from the wheels. High above rich vegetation crowns the top of the mountains. Adam's Peak, owing to the heavy moisture, was not to be seen. The Bible Rock stands out in bold relief on the other side of the valley.

Shortly after passing this wonderful place we arrived at Kandy, the nominal capital of the island, but in reality the seat of government is Colombo. I noticed here the grand acacia trees, their beautiful quivering leaves showing dark and rich in the humid atmosphere, and I repeat, as I have always said, a small acacia, well grown and properly managed, is far ahead of many others as a table-plant. The damp air, the flies, and the dust make it next to impossible to write. Kandy is a straggling native town, high up in an upland valley, rich in foliage. The Queen's Hotel produced a very jolly lunch. A visit to the Temple of Buddha (where the old gentleman's tooth is preserved), a stroll through the market, where natives chew the beetle-nut, and allow the vermilion stain to trickle from the mouth over their dusky skin. The police court is a curious place, and no Cingalee is thought of any importance unless he has at least one case always before the court.

We were bound to start at two on the return journey, to avoid any chance of missing the ship. I was glad to avail myself of information very simply and pleasantly given by Mr. H——, a planter of some years' standing. The scenery on the homeward journey was, of course, simply reversed.

Nothing I hope will ever efface such beautiful pictures from my memory—the hundreds of shades of brilliant green, lighted up by red flashes of Pointcettia or pointed Dracœna, the herds of tame buffalo, the groups of natives, the jungle-tree with its bunches of tulip-shaped flowers, the humid atmosphere heavy in moist heat, put me in mind of old Gatcombe stove-house, and, as you will remember, many of the flowers I have named were there. I know you will all be tired long before you get to this.

A good dinner and a dance ended a very pleasant and interesting day. Colombo with its red streets and white blinding houses, would no doubt have been very full of novelty, but time did not allow of much exploration. The jewellers and curio dealers are without exception the most awful rascals in the world—they will readily ask £75 for a ring, and then take 5s. The quantity of Birmingham jewellery imported here is fabulous; of course there are plenty of good stones to be bought—and bought reasonably, and under the guidance of Dr. R——, a man who has bought £700 at one time and another, I managed to get a ring or so. The snake-charmer is here in full force, the reptiles crawl all over him, or fight with the mangoose—for the amusement (?) of travellers.

Having paid a fairly reasonable bill, we drove to the landing stage, and soon found ourselves on board the *Carthage*, in the midst of a babel of noise, dust, dirt, heat and confusion. It is quite beyond human power to convey to others the scene on board a P. and O. ship in Colombo

Harbour. The natives crowd round the ship in the native catamaran, a narrow boat, with a huge fixed wooden outrigger; these dusky gentry swarm over the sides with fruit, sticks, jewellery, lace (fresh from Nottingham), precious stones (straight from the glass-works), tortoise-shell work, Indian silver-work, ebony elephants, and every variety of rubbish—all haggling at once, shouting and laughing; the noisy crane moving, the donkey engine going, the great heat, the coal dust, the closed ports, and you may be sure I was glad to see the deck cleared of these dirty rascals, to feel the old screw revolve, and once more to steam away in our floating hotel. In a few hours, low-lying Colombo was a thing of the past. Don't buy stones here unless you have somebody who *really* knows something about them. Streeter, of Bond Street, has a place here, but at *London prices.* Silva & Co. are also to be trusted. Cingalee tea is pungent and good.

Sunday, 23rd Dec.—Just fancy! only two days to Christmas day, doubtless with you heralded in with snow. I picture you all looking forward to A——, A——, and P——'s visit. I can picture the little preparations for the holiday, and B——'s Christmas tree. We crossed the equator to-day, at a little before noon; being Sunday, no fun or demonstration took place, in fact, the old-fashioned frolic of King Neptune has gone out of date with the rapid service of modern times. The heat under double awnings is about 85° in the coolest part of the ship. This heat is very moist; everybody gets gluey and sticky, but on the whole, we have every reason for being more than thankful.

Last night, L—— and I got on deck at 4 a.m., to see the Southern Cross, and this time the constellation was no fraud; the moon was at the quarter, and intensely bright. It is quite beyond me to portray the brilliancy of the stars; of course, the great bear and other old friends are away from us. Attended morning and evening service. I fancy I mentioned that a Dr. R—— put me on to buying some stones at Colombo—the home of the sapphire. We had been talking of snakes, snakes, all the evening, and, of *course*, I must go and dream of the nasty reptiles, and awake with the impression that a big cobra was quietly coiled on my chest. I was on my back asleep, and a heavy woollen shirt must have fallen from the rack on my chest; the heat caused thereby gave this horrid nightmare—the very thought of it is *real* even now.

24th Dec.—Hot and muggy, and I can safely say—

> "There is nothing on board half so sweet as a plunge,
> In a jolly big bath, with a jolly big sponge."

I am sorry to state that one of the passengers, P——T——, did exactly the same as I did, viz., strike his head against the lintel, but *far more severely;* for concussion of the brain and a scalp wound were the result. He is conscious now, but we all fear he may suffer. We saw a water-spout to-day coiling darkly about a mile ahead; it dispersed suddenly, and immediately after we got in for a real tropical shower— huge drops nearly touching each other; all more or less wet through before we could gain shelter. The normal condition of a diary-man is want of news—no oracle or spirit-rapper on board. Some ladies think the men on board the *Carthage* prefer their "horrid pipes and smoking-room chat to flirting and gossiping with them in the manner proper to the Southern ocean." One lady told me she thought most of the men on board were "quiet men." I always have my kettle-drum with Mrs. B—— and Mrs. F——. (I find she only lost her husband about three months ago; she is very quiet and nice, about twenty-three). Writing on board ship in the tropics is really a species of "mental gymnastics," equal in effect to waltzing in a Turkish bath. The phosphorus last night was very bright, and in these latitudes strikes the beholder with wonder and admiration. It prevails in nearly all temperate waters, but shows to fullest extent in the tropical seas, and proceeds from a great variety of minute organisms, some soft and gelatinous, others of minute "crustacea."

A Christmas Day on the Indian Ocean.

25th Dec.—At breakfast nearly all the men came out in clean white flannels, or white cotton suits, the ladies in light or white dresses, all looking cool, fresh and bright, and nearly every plate had at least one, and many a bundle of Christmas cards, brought away from loved ones at home, and sacredly kept until the day; my letter and beautiful card was duly appreciated.

A short service at ten brought nearly all the passengers together. Then the quarter-masters carried the Captain and each of the officers round the deck in a chair, covered with the Union Jack, the band playing and the men singing "For he's a jolly good fellow." At one we sat down to a capital lunch, and how they ever cooked so many large and really first-class dishes will always remain a mystery to me. The cakes were made on board, and weighed 60 lbs. each, and stood over 3 feet high, and were virtually wedding cakes, decorated with holly and mistletoe: and what with pines, pomelas, oranges, pears, apples, ices, and tarts representing the flag of the P. and O. service, &c., custard, black currant jam, red currant jam, and marmalade—making black, white, yellow and red.

DINNER.

Soup.
Mock Turtle.   Clear Spring.

Fish.
Boiled Turbot and Lobster Sauce.
Salmon Cutlets, a la Madras.

Entrees.
Jugged Hare.
Green Peas, a la Bonne Hemme.   Mutton Cutlets, a la Vicomtesse.
Petit Bonches, a la Financiere.

Joints, &c.
Roast Sirloin Beef.   Roast Turkey and Sausages.
Chicken Curry.

Pastry, &c.
Plum Pudding.   Mince Pies.
Tipsy Cakes.   Ice Puddings.

HEAT 82° IN SHADE.

After a little rest and smoke, the athletic sports commenced. The obstacle race was hard work, and a rare bit of fun. The competitors had to go from one end of the deck to the other, and back again. The 1st obstacle was through three life-buoys swinging on a rope; 2nd, over a high pole securely tied *close* to roof of awning; 3rd, a rope fixed *very tight*, six inches from the deck; 4th, to crawl through the windows of the engine-room; 5th, get to top and run over the engine-room; 6th, creep through a long wind-sail; 7th, over a wire rope; 8th, under a low form; 9th, over an oar on end close to awning. This repeated, was jolly stiff work; two or three gave up—many knocks and cuts were received, and a little fainting gave variety. I acted as nurse, tying up, plastering, bathing, brandying and sodaing patients. The tournament followed:— Men on "pick-a-back," trying to dismount one another, more frequently they rolled down in one confused heap. The potato race—20 potatoes placed at regular intervals on the deck, each to be fetched and deposited in a bucket. The spoon and potato race—each competitor with a dessert spoon held between his teeth, holding a potato; any man dropping the potato would of necessity lose the race. The tug-of-war finished the entertainment. I can assure you my afternoon tub was most refreshing. Most dress suits for the evening ball consisted of blue yachting suits and white vests. We danced from 8.30 to 11.30. The dinner, with its Christmas cheer, the toasts of the Queen, Captain, &c., was very enjoyable. Curiously enough, "absent friends" was drank at 8.30, just before going to the ball-room, and that was 2.30 at home. A quiet pipe finished my first Christmas day at sea—a well-mixed day of orthodox fun and good fellowship.

26th Dec.—Upon looking out of my port, I noticed the sea to be covered with broad streaks of some yellowish drab substance. L—— at once put it down to be pumice stone, for large pieces frequently passed the ship, and the open pores were visible. We at once connected this curious sight with the Island of Java, where earthquakes and eruptions have lately so torn up and desolated the place. Being only some 1,500 miles from there, the N.E. trade-wind and the current had carried the light substance with it. In appearance it was exactly like the *top* of Vesuvias. This has been a quiet day, and half the dancing men were sound asleep before noon. My intellectual excitement consisted in reading a rubbishy novel.

27th Dec.—N.E. trade-winds are blowing dead ahead, making the ship nice and fresh, and bracing us up. I can assure you we all more or less feel flabby, and to a certain extent nerveless. We have about three dozen mangoose on board, shipped for Australia, to help clear the rabbit pest. By-the-bye, we have a man called Austin on board; his grandfather was the first to introduce the rabbit to the colony. The piano is no unmixed blessing, for it is going ALL day long.

ODE TO THE PIANO BY A PASSENGER (NOT ME).

    Tinkle, tinkle, all day long,
    First a piece, and then a song;
      Seldom anything that's new,
      Seldom time or touch are true.

    Tinkle, tinkle, night and day—
    How I wish some folks that play
      Would try and learn the proper way,
      Or silent let the piano stay.

I won another sweep to-day, making my total winnings exactly £18, 18s., and again to-day L—— took the second prize. No mosquitoes at present, but no end of cockroaches have taken up their quarters in the smoking-room. I still admire the *Carthage*. The parson can do a very quiet walk to-day, and most of the invalids are better, but warm muggy air cannot do otherwise than unbrace the system. We run something under 300 miles in the twenty-four hours. We fear it will be nearly a week before we see King George's Sound, for the head wind pulls us back. A mangoose ate his way through the wooden box to-day, and created a scare, for the mangoose is supposed to be very fond of new baby, and we have four or five on board.

28th Dec.—Nothing to say, nothing done, although a beautiful and bracing day. The same deep blue sea. A most peculiar sunset, with *deep orange-coloured clouds*, fringed with bright gold. The superstitious Hindoos when they saw it were alarmed, and thought the last day, or something, was coming, and whenever you met a Lascar he looked quite upset. I must admit it had a weird appearance. Sirius is very bright here.

SYDNEY—

Population, 220,427. Distance from London, 12,136. Local time, 10 hrs. 5 m. before Greenwich. *Present* cost of telegram to England, 10s. 10d. per word.

560, SYDNEY to MELBOURNE—

Population, 282,981. Distance from London, 11,566. Local time, before Greenwich, 9.40. 10s. 8d. per word.

ADELAIDE—

Population, 37,892. Distance from London, 10,074. 9.14 before Greenwich.

COLOMBO to KING GEORGE'S SOUND 3,390—
Distance from London, 6,703 miles.

29th Dec.—As usual! Beautiful weather; a slight roll. At 8.30 P.M. the stewards gave us a very good nigger entertainment—the bones and banjo were exceptional performers, and many of the glees were well rendered. Clog dancing and jokes were excellent. I will try and remember one or two of the riddles:—

"Why is our noble Captain like old Port?—Because the older he gets the better we like him."

"How is it the Captain of the *Carthage* is never lonely?

—Because he has a companion in his cabin (companion stair)."

"What is the difference between a glass of ale and a glass of water?—2d. (twopence)."

"Why does the *Carthage* resemble a silk handkerchief?—Because she has stood many a good blow."

"How is it our noble doctor resembles a dead duck?—Because he has no quack in him."

"Why is a lady's silver belt like a dust-cart?—Because it goes round and gathers in the waist."

"What is the difference between a lady and an umbrella?—One you *can* shut up; try the other."

"Why do the stewards of the *Carthage* resemble race horses?—Because they clear cups, plates, steaks, and gallop over the courses."

"Why do so many of the unmarried ladies like the climate of Ceylon?—Because there are so many single he's there! (Cingalees)."

The concert was on deck, the stage raised, and separated by a running curtain, the enclosure covered with flags of all nations, and the space capable of holding 150. "God save the Queen," by all, ended a pleasant evening.

Sunday, the 30th Dec.—The sixth Sunday at sea. Awoke to the rise and fall of a heavy swell. The ship rolling from 10 to 12 degrees. Beautiful, fresh, bracing day; vests and underclothing resumed, and in the evening stroll greatcoats were used. Here it is that careless people get colds; some greet with a sneer of contempt the advice, "beware of the cold evenings!" Very nice service, and a sermon of six and a quarter minutes by the Rev. Archdeacon Dove. The rev. gentleman and I have got quite chatty; he got on board at Colombo, having passed the last six months in India, and we have enjoyed many a good yarn about Italy and India, and, wonderful to say, he quite agrees with me that religion should be self-supporting.

31st Dec.—The last day of 1883. One of the most glorious days I ever remember—fine, bracing, and sunny. Everybody in for enjoyment, and it will be long before I forget the New-Year's Eve of 1883—songs, "Auld Lang Syne," and, sad to tell, numerous whiskies, finished a year full of many incidents. Won first and second prize in sweep to-day, value £9.

1st Jan., 1884.—I cannot do better than give some idea of this grand ship, the *Carthage*. Built by Caird & Co., of Greenock (Glasgow), at a cost of £160,000, 5,000 horse-power, and 5,013 tons; she can carry 157 first-class and 46 second. *No steerage.* In fact, the 46 second are really meant only for servants of the first class. The first-class passengers' place, or hurricane-deck, is 212 feet in length, and here it is we stroll up and down, smoke, read, &c. She draws 26 to 27 feet water, and beam 48. The saloon can dine in *perfect* comfort 148. Her average speed is 300 miles a-day, but I do not think her a fast boat. Mrs. B—— and myself went over the engine-room to-day. They are compound engines of the Tandem type (*i.e.*, one on the top of another), and beautifully kept. The ice-house and refrigerator are very useful, but a terrible affair took place a voyage or two ago. The butcher was by accident shut in the ice-room, and some hours after he was found frozen to death. I made a snowball from the frozen water (or rather air). The best cabins for men in this ship *going* to Australia are the post-office cabins (spar deck), *starboard* side, or 102, 103, 104 (*for two*). 69, 70 (ours), on port side, are good. Always select cabins on starboard side *going* and port *returning*. The crew consists of captain, six officers, eight quartermasters (all English), and 50 Lascars (sailors), and 50 seedy boys (stokers, firemen, and engineers' attendants), one chief engineer, and six assistant engineers. The Lascar is a British subject, and means sea-faring Hindoo. Altogether they are fine seamen for hot climates, but our cold at home tries them very much during the short time they are there. These Lascars enter the P. and O. service from 10 to 12 years of age, and then act as punkah boys, and gradually rise. The best Lascars come from Gogo or Surat. The stewards number 38, and are all sharp, clean, well-disposed men.

Have again won the second prize in the sweep—£3, and L—— £3. My winnings have now amounted to £30, but that you may easily imagine is not all profit, and the phiz (or fiz) it cost is something considerable; and, what with gifts to organs, seamen's homes, &c., I fear I shall not have much to thank my luck for, although it is altogether unprecedented. I have won three first, four second, and half a first out of 13 sweeps, and 50 entries each time. By the thoughtful kindness that runs through and underlies the administration of affairs on board this beautiful vessel, we have a grand lunch to-day —boar's head, large cakes, &c., and in short every luxury you can think of, and our dinner to-night is to be something quite out of the common. We all had a cheery new-year's greeting for each other, and the bright, fresh day, the dancing blue waves, the song of the thrush, the briskness engendered by the bracing atmosphere, has given new life to all on board. We expect to be at King George's Sound (Australia) to-morrow at eight p.m. All are more or less excited. We have a dance to-night on deck, but the theatrical performance comes off on Thursday and Friday, and Saturday is to be dedicated to a fancy dress ball, so I don't think to-night's dance will be up to much. It was not up to anything.

2nd Jan.—Got on deck about eight, and the bare, barren rocks of Western Australia were seen on the starboard bow quite close to us. We sailed abreast the low rocky coast all day long. The Lascars hard at work getting up bales, casks of coffee, &c., for King George's Sound. The punkahs are now put away as useless, and the fresh air is quite invigorating. The invalids are mostly on deck, and even now I don't know the names of some few of our fellow-passengers. After dinner, and just as we were all going ashore to see the small town of Albany, two telegrams were placed in my hand—one directed to L—— and one to myself. I at once thought of dear F—— and others at home, but another sheet will tell the sad, sad tale.

3rd Jan.—Some terribly sad news quite upset the ship and altered our plans.

Theatricals, tableaux, took place in the evening, but I cannot tell you what they were, for I did not go. Part of the saloon was made into a regular stage.

4th Jan.—Very cold indeed; a regular draught through the ship, and sneezing the order of the day. Nothing particular, and for the most part we amused ourselves by watching the flight of the albatross. Wax-works and theatricals during the evening—both of high merit.

WAX-WORK FIGURES—

Little Bo-Peep. The Spotted Baby from Peru. Vivandiere. Nancy Lee. Daniel and the Lions (Daniel with a *Times* newspaper and a topper-hat). Irish Squire. Gipsy Flower Girl. Bushman. Rule Britannia. Showman and Joe (the winder up).

DONE ON BOTH SIDES (*Farce*).

This was well acted by nearly all the artists. B——, the parson, had a flash character, and he frequently used the expressive, but hardly clerical damn, and many think he should have selected another impersonation; but, wherever you go, you find the cloth try and adapt their religion to the social requirements and conditions by which they are surrounded. All are in grand excitement, preparing for the ball; this, the last dance, is to be in fancy dress, and a lot of amusement is anticipated. The gets-up will be very extraordinary. One lady is coming out as the Captain, dressed in the full dress uniform of Captain Hector. Another (at my suggestion) as the baby, but I will try and remember them to-morrow. This being the last dinner we can all possibly spend together, speeches and an address to the Captain will be gone into. A good many get out at Adelaide, so after to-night the voyage is virtually at an end.

5th Jan.—Landed about 8.30 at Glenelg, the P. and O. Port of Adelaide, but did not find young L—— as anticipated; so took cars to Adelaide, a distance of 6 miles, and after some time found him at the York Hotel. The Post-Office is really a grand building, the streets are very wide and well laid out; many of the public buildings far surpass ours at home. The country at this time of year has a very dried-up look, and one can hardly realise that cattle can thrive on such stuff, but they do. The best building sites in Adelaide fetch as much as £600 *per foot frontage.* We went over the botanical gardens, and were introduced to Dr. S——, the curator. Returned in time for lunch; three o'clock saw us quietly steaming away. I ought to mention that the weeping willow at Adelaide grows more luxuriously than I could have imagined it possible, and the variety of pine trees most astonishing. The India-rubber (ficus) grow here rapidly, and are generally used to form groves on each side of the street. Soon after leaving, the old *Carthage* began to roll in a most determined manner, the clinometer registering from 28° to 32°. Over 100 glasses were smashed at one lurch, and many an interesting tableaux took place on deck. Music and cards, &c.

The *6th Jan.*—Did nothing but grumble.

7th Jan.—Still the same heavy roll, and packing was next to impossible under the circumstances, but it had to be done. I got everything in, but *how*, I won't say. I was invited to dine with the R—— at the *side* table; and I shall never forget that dinner—our fiddles were made for mid-ships, not for the side tables; glasses, tumblers, soup, fruits, &c., whisked away in one melee, and then as suddenly sent flying back again. This lasted for an hour and a-half, and how many plates, glasses, &c., were smashed, I cannot say. I christened this dinner a "Charge of the Light Brigade." We said adieu to the Captain and all we cared about. A jolly party in the smoking-room finished a voyage of 48 days made nearly in fine weather, and, taken all in all, the passengers were kind, well-bred, and pleasant.

Tuesday, 8th Jan.—Landed in great confusion. After much trouble, we got all luggage passed, and safe at Scott's (the best place for men). L—— and I were made members of the Melbourne and Australian Clubs. Owing to the sad news, we shall go over to New Zealand at once, and all our plans are somewhat upset—11,585 miles, 47 days 7 hours, P. and O. Steamer.

MELBOURNE.

Hotels.—Scott's for gentlemen, Oriental and Menzies for families. Australian and Melbourne Clubs, both high-class, exceptionally good. Population about 300,000. Some of the buildings are very fine, notably the new Law Courts. Collins Street, Elizabeth Street, and Bourke Street are well built, and nearly all streets are at right angles. Fitzroy and Botanical Gardens are beautifully laid out. Race-course simply perfection, and the cricket-ground unique for comfort and size.

The climate of Melbourne is one of the most changeable in the world, and it is no uncommon thing to see mornings of bright, hot sunshine, with a scorching wind, change within a few hours to afternoons of a biting cold, when the strongest are thankful for ulsters or sealskin jackets. On the hottest days people may be seen carrying heavy coats or rugs in anticipation of the sudden change of weather that may occur—a gentleman living here gave me this information.

UNION STEAMSHIP COMPANY'S FLEET.

	Gross Reg.	I.H.P.	Built.		Gross Reg.	I.H.P.	Built.
Rotomahana,	1727	2000	1879	Hero,	985	750	1861
Tarawera,	2003	1750	1882	Penguin,	749	900	1864
Waihora,	2003	1750	1882	Hawea,	721	850	1875
Wairarapa,	1786	1750	1882	Wanaka,	493	600	1876
Manapouri,	1783	1750	1882	Omapere,	601	500	1882
Hauroto,	1988	1500	1882	Taiaroa,	438	500	1875
Te Anau,	1652	1500	1879	Mahinapua,	423	500	1882
Wakatipu,	1797	1250	1876	Suva,	293	250	1876
Arawata,	1098	1250	1875	Southern Cross,	282	250	1873
Ringarooma,	1096	1250	1875	Maori,	174	250	1867
Takapuna,	930	2000	1883	Beautiful Star,	177	150	1862
Rotorua,	926	900	1876	Waihi,	92	100	1882

SERVICES.

Intercolonial Services.

The steamers of the company leave Melbourne weekly for all New Zealand ports, calling at Hobart every alternate trip. They also make weekly departures from Sydney for New Zealand, *via* Auckland and East Coast ports, and fortnightly *via* Cook Strait and Wellington. In addition, a steamer is despatched from Melbourne once a month for Suva and Levuka (Fiji), and another from Auckland (New Zealand) for the same ports.

Coastal Services.

The coastal services include weekly steamers from Dunedin (Port Chalmers) to Auckland, *via* East Coast ports, and *vice versa;* and to Manukau, *via* intermediate ports, and *vice versa;* twice weekly between Wellington and Nelson, and three times a week between Wellington and Lyttelton each way. In addition to these, there are services twice a week between Dunedin and Timaru each way: between Dunedin and Oamaru each way, and weekly between Dunedin and West Coast of Middle Island; while a special steamer runs regularly between Wellington and Auckland, *via* Gisborne and Napier, leaving each terminal port on alternate Mondays.

Express Service.

A new and special feature of the excursion season of 1883–84 is the initiation of an express passenger and mail service on the coast, by means of the company's new swift and powerful s.s. *Takapuna*, particulars of which will be found in the notice of excursion season arrangements.

15th Jan.—Got on board the *Wairarapa*, Union S.S. Company, at three o'clock, after a struggle. She is a new boat. The numerous passengers and their friends literally swarmed the deck. This steamer is without exception the most finished specimen of forethought and ingenuity I have ever seen. Electric light all over the place, with a provision in case of failure of the most perfect oil-lamps. She was built by Denny Brothers, of Dumbarton, in 1882. Size 1,786 tons; horse-power, 1,700. The saloon, social hall, and smoking-rooms were simply superb. The unfortunate part of the whole affair for us was that she carried 130 first-class instead of 50, and only 250 tons instead of 1,700. Of course we got in for a regular tossing. A heavy beam sea, interspersed with fierce squalls, set the ship rolling. L——, son, and self were packed with one other into a cabin not large enough for two—no room for bags or anything, and right up in the bows. Many slept in the passages. Altogether, the five days' voyage was simply horrid, the very life nearly rolled out of us, and, although not actually sick, we all three felt ill effects. On the morning of Sunday we steamed slowly into Milford Sound. When fairly abreast of the entrance, the Mitre Peak (5,500 feet) came in sight, and though 1,000 feet lower than Pembroke Peak (6,700), it is a fitting companion for the latter, standing as they do one on either side of the entrance. Where lay the passage it was hard to tell, for we looked as if steaming on to an unbroken cliff till we suddenly rounded a point and found ourselves right inside this gorgeous sound, putting me in mind of the entrance to Christiansund (Norway).

NEW ZEALAND.

It is quite unnecessary for me to remind you that Captain Cook was the first Englishman who, to our knowledge, landed in New Zealand (1769), but the country was discovered by a Dutchman 100 years before that, named Abel Tasman—hence Tasmania. The native Maories are, no doubt, of Polynesian origin, and tradition points to the Navigator Group as the most direct connection. The race, now gradually dying out, have many good qualities—they are brave, generous, and very good humoured, and fond of their children; they give away things cheerfully, and accept them in the same manner, but never thank you for a gift—in fact, they have no word in their language to express that meaning. The New Zealand bush is very fine indeed, and there are more than 100 different kinds of forest trees—the tallest and most useful being the kauri, which often grows to 150 feet; it is beautiful in foliage and valuable as timber; it produces an amber kind of gum, but it grows only in the North Island—here this gum is found in great quantities under the ground where Kauri forests have once stood.

The rata is also a beautiful and curious plant; it is a rope-like vine finding its "origin and support" in other trees, which at last it presses to death, and the rata itself becomes a strong and sturdy tree, bearing most beautiful scarlet blossoms. We were rather late for the bloom, but, nevertheless, saw and gathered some splendid bits.

A great curiosity is often dug out at the foot of the rata; it looks, and doubtless is, a dead caterpillar, with a sort of fungus like a bullrush growing out of its head, and from this stem the young rata tree is formed, at least so a man who sold us some specimens said. The ferns of New Zealand are so well known that I will say nothing but this, that no more charming sight can be imagined than an undergrowth of these lovely plants; 130 different varieties are to be found here. There is nothing to fear in these cool and dark forests, with their carpet of soft green moss and fern, for snakes and wild animals are totally absent. A solemn silence adds another peculiar charm.

This country is rich in minerals, and few can even estimate what New Zealand contains. Gold has been found in Otago, Westland, Nelson, and Hokitiki. Silver is found in Nelson and Otago. Coal is found in great quantities in many parts, chiefly in the Bay of Islands in the north, Grey River in Westland, and the region of the Waikato River. L—— and I visited the iron works outside Auckland, and saw the iron-sand—a curiosity very interesting to both. It is of good quality, and practically inexhaustible, but the works are at a stand-still.

Greenstone is found in Westland, lead is found in Nelson and Otago, zinc in Auckland and Nelson, quicksilver in the Bay of Islands. Excellent building stone in many parts. There appear to be about 150 different kinds of birds, the most curious being the wingless moa, standing from 10 to 14 feet in height, now extinct. We saw a fine specimen at the Christ Church Museum. Another strange wingless bird called kiwi, is every now and again to be found alive. There are many varieties of parrots, and some paraquets.

The tui, or parson bird, called so from a bunch of white feathers under the neck, is easily taught to talk. The swamps, lakes, and rivers abound in wild duck, and the angler can have the finest fishing in the Southern Hemisphere, its creeks and rivers are literally teeming with fish, and various acclimatisation societies have brought salmon and trout hatching to perfection. Trout fishing season begins October 1st and ends 31st March. They are very large, but will not take the fly in Lake Wakatipu. Hares and pheasants can be found, but the latter are faring very badly owing to the poisoned grain being placed about to get rid of the rabbits. By-the-bye, I must not forget to mention the (phormium tenax) or flax plant, it is to be seen nearly all over the islands; I fear the cost of preparation will never make it a paying article of commerce. If you see the flax growing, you may fairly suppose the soil to be good. All the above little bits of information have been picked up from observation, books, or gossip. The climate of New Zealand, taken as a whole, is as good, if not better, than any in the world, although the winds are sometimes boisterous, and rains heavy.

The following extracts are copied verbatim from the *Handbook of the Auckland Agricultural Company (Limited)*:—

"And first as to climate and soil. There is no doubt that in this respect New Zealand has great advantages for agricultural purposes over the other colonies. Lying as it does between 34° 30′ and 47° 30′ it is evident that, while it must contain a great variety of climate, there cannot at ordinary altitudes be any great excess of heat or cold. The climate of New Zealand, taken as a whole, is the best in the world. Dr. Hector, in his handbook, page 51, thus describes the temperature:—

"'The climate resembles that of Great Britain, but is more equable, the extremes of daily temperature only varying throughout the year by an average of 20°, whilst London is 7° colder than the North, and 4° colder than the South Island of New Zealand. The mean annual temperature of the North Island is 57°, and of the South Island 52°; that of London and New York being 51°. The mean annual temperature of the different seasons for the whole colony is, in spring 55°, in summer 63°, in autumn 57°, and in winter 48°.'

"The rainfall returns for Auckland are given :—

Winter.	Spring.	Summer.	Autumn.	Total for Year.
32	25	19	24	47·008 ins.

"Probability of rain :—

Winter.	Spring.	Summer.	Autumn.	Year.	Mean Maximum in 24 hours.
0·61	0·52	0·33	0·41	0·47	3·358

"Abstract of comparative temperature taken over observations of twenty years at Auckland :—

S. Lat.	Longitude East.	No. of years observation.	Year.	Winter.	Spring.	Summer.	Autumn.
36·50	174·51	20	59·50	52·34	57·56	66·92	61·16

Difference of coldest and warmest months.	Yearly Means.		Yearly Fluctuations.
	Maximum.	Minimum.	
16·02	88·52	33·26	55·26

"The following figures show the comparative births and deaths in New Zealand, as compared with the other colonies in Australasia :—

	Rate per 1,000 of Population.		
	Deaths.	Births.	Excess of Births over Deaths.
New Zealand, ...	$12\frac{2}{3}$	$41\frac{2}{3}$	230
Western Australia, . . .	$14\frac{1}{6}$	34	140
South Australia, ...	$16\frac{1}{2}$	$37\frac{3}{4}$	132
Victoria, ...	$16\frac{1}{3}$	$32\frac{1}{4}$	98
Tasmania, ...	$16\frac{1}{8}$	30	82
New South Wales, . . .	18	$37\frac{2}{3}$	108
Queensland, ...	$18\frac{3}{4}$	$37\frac{1}{2}$	99

"The subjoined statistical table, copied from the *Sydney Morning Herald*, is also interesting and valuable. It speaks strongly, though unconsciously, by the force of official figures and returns, in favour of New Zealand. 'What,' asks that journal, 'is Australasia doing towards meeting the world's demand for bread? To answer that, we have constructed the following table, which our readers may find useful in its application to many questions now agitating the public mind in this colony:—

WHEAT-GROWING IN AUSTRALASIA.

	Cultivated.	Under Wheat.	Yield of Wheat.
	Acres.	Acres.	Bushels.
New South Wales,	513,840	145,609	2,391,979
Victoria,	1,231,105	401,417	5,279,730
South Australia,	1,514,916	1,083,732	5,857,569
New Zealand,	2,940,711	141,614	4,143,540
Total,	6,200,572	1,772,372	17,672,818

"The pre-eminence of New Zealand in this is remarkably manifest, as the subjoined calculations, given in a recast form, and showing the yield of wheat per acre in each colony, fully demonstrated. The average yield from 1,772,000 acres is just a fraction under 10 bushels per acre. The individual production per acre in each colony is as under:—

	Average yield per annum.
New Zealand,	29½ bushels.
New South Wales,	16½ ,,
Victoria,	13 ,,
South Australia,	5½ ,,

"Which colony then carries away the palm? Undoubtedly New Zealand. She produced per acre nearly three times the general average of the whole of the four colonies. She has nearly double the yield of New South Wales; she gives two and a third times the produce per acre that Victoria can boast, and almost five and a half times the quantity which South Australia yields.

"The following extract from a speech delivered by Sir Hercules

Robinson, K.C.M.G., the late Governor of New Zealand, will also be read with interest :—

"'And now allow me to say that the first impressions which I have formed of New Zealand are most favourable. I have already, in the few months I have been here, visited most of the principal centres of population—from Auckland in the north to Invercargill in the south—and I can truly say that the country appears to me to be of surpassing interest and promise. The scenery is quite equal, if not superior to anything I have seen in any other part of the world. I have been much struck also with the extent and variety of the resources of the country, as well as with the industry and energy, and marvellous rapidity with which they are being developed. (Hear, hear.) Coming from Australia, I could not fail to note with admiration the extraordinary richness of the soil, and its special adaptability for homestead settlement upon comparatively small areas. (Cheers.) Your climate, too, is magnificent—far more enjoyable than that of the old country; whilst it is equally favourable to the development of British energy. The influence of climate and soil is, I think, clearly perceptible upon the physical development and character of the population, for wherever I have travelled I have found men brimful of energy, cheerful and contented with their lot, believing thoroughly in the land of their adoption and determined to promote her advancement to a foremost place among the dependencies of the British Crown. (Cheers.) I know of no sight more calculated to impress an Englishman with feelings of pride and thankfulness than to travel through a great new country like this, which was only first settled about forty years ago, and to see on all sides the evidence which it affords of material progress and social improvement. To see great cities like Christchurch, Dunedin, Wellington, Auckland, and Invercargill, which have grown up as if by magic—to see, as I did, mountains of grain stacked and waiting shipment at Omaru and Timaru, the produce of districts which a few years ago did not grow enough for their own consumption—to see such a pastoral and agricultural show as I inspected to-day, and of which many of the old countries of Europe might well feel proud—to see everywhere vast districts of country which twenty-five years ago were unproductive, covered with flocks and herds, and corn fields, and administering to the wants and contributing to the happiness of hundreds of thousands of our race—I say such sights as these make one feel proud of the genius of our countrymen for colonisation, and confident as to the future of this great country. (Cheers.) The resources of the land are boundless; it is capable of supporting in comfort and independence a population of many millions, and it offers, to my mind, on the whole, more advantages than any other country in the world with which I am acquainted to industrious and hard-working men. (Cheers.) Nature has indeed been most bountiful to New Zealand. She has given her beautiful scenery, a magnificent climate, a soil of unsurpassed fertility, and extensive seaboard, a commanding position, and in short, every natural condition necessary for the reproduction here on these southern seas of a younger and happier Britain, exempt from the stint and want and the misery which are unfortunately so common at times in the old country, and offering a far more general participation in the good gifts which God has so bountifully bestowed on this country.'" (Loud cheers.)

" The total area of New Zealand is about 64,000,000 acres, of which about 12,000,000 acres are suitable for agriculture, about 30,000,000 are better suited for pastoral purposes, and about 20,000,000 acres, of which a large area when cleared will make good land, are covered with forest.

"The question of labour, which is generally considered to be the great drawback to profitable farming in any new country, and which especially concerns the 'all-round' farmer, to whom the price at which the various operations of agriculture can be done is of the greatest importance.

"It does not so much matter to the Canterbury or Otago sheep farmer, or the grazier in the North Island, for when once a farm, in the Waikato district, for instance, is properly fenced and sown down with grass, the labour connected with it is trifling. A little ploughing here and there, as the plant of clover begins to fail, the sowing of a field of turnips, as extra feed in the winter, and the branding of the cattle, which, in a properly-made stock-yard, is not a very difficult matter, is almost all the labour that is required. One or two hired men, besides the master, who must expect to do some work himself, will be sufficient for a 1,000-acre grazing farm, where there is no housing of cattle in winter, or feeding with artificial food.

"Sheep, too, in the runs especially, require very little looking after, and a couple of men will be ample for a run of many thousand sheep, except at the mustering and clipping seasons.

"But, after all, the question still remains unanswered: Is New Zealand a good field of emigration for British tenant-farmers? Will they be able to use there, to advantage, the capital that remains to them after the hard times through which we have been passing, and will they be able there to establish the home which an Englishman, in whatever part of the world he lives, wishes to possess? We answer 'yes' to all these. We believe that any English farmer, of industry and perseverance, possessing a little capital, and a good knowledge of his business, may make a very good living for himself and his family, and will have better opportunities of settling his children than he would in a country like ours, which, after centuries of occupation, is crowded in every corner with members of every trade, profession, and calling.

"We wish to be understood: he must not think that by going to New Zealand he is stepping into a fortune; steadiness and industry are necessary elements of success there as here, but are more sure of their reward. To have made the fortunes and amassed the large landed estates which he will see around him, he should have been there years ago, when the swamps were undrained and the roads unmade, when he must have crossed every torrent that flows from the Southern Alps at the risk of being swept away, or slept at night in fear of having his throat cut by the Maories before morning. These dangers are practically gone now: every river is not bridged, but many are ; the natives, where they exist in any numbers in districts settled by Englishmen, are rather useful than otherwise.

"It is a mistake, into which people at home not uncommonly fall, to think that New Zealand is all alike, and that it does not much matter to what part they direct their steps, as the same sort of country and occupation will meet them at all places. From what we have said it will be seen that this is altogether a wrong idea. There are in the colony greater varieties of soil, of climate, and of agricultural occupations, if we may so term them, than it would be easy to find in any other country of the same size.

"It depends altogether upon what sort of farming a man prefers; and he can have his choice of almost any kind. If a warm climate with mild winters suits him, and he wishes to devote himself to cattle and sheep breeding, this can be done to perfection in the Waikato district of the North Island and the Thames Valley, and we thoroughly believe that it is a profitable field of labour. It is a good place for a man of capital who wishes to acquire a large freehold at a comparatively low price, and when once the stock is bought and the farm got into cultivation, it can be worked at a low cost, owing to the small amount of care and attention required by live stock in that favoured climate. On the other hand, a man of small capital, desirous of carrying on his farm by the united labour of himself and his family only, should do very well in the same district for the same reasons. And one enormous advantage the freeholder in a new colony possesses is this : that year by year, while he plods along making his yearly returns, his land is silently but steadily increasing in value by the progress of settlement around and beyond him, and the regular growth of the colony ; and in this way, even if not by annual returns from his stock and farming operations, he is certain to add to his wealth, as hundreds of settlers in New Zealand have done before.

"The following extracts from a little work called *Farming in North New Zealand*, by the Rev. J. Berry, are interesting as corroborating what we have advanced :—

"'During a twelve years' residence I have never seen ice there which would bear a child, nor snow three inches deep, except on the mountains. Deep snow and ice thick enough for skating may be found in the extreme south, but not often, and no settler need go there who is anxious to avoid these. Sheep and cattle and horses live and prosper in the open air all the year round. The days are very few, even in winter, in which a delicate person may not enjoy a walk or ride in the open air.

"' New Zealand has no rainy season in the sense in which the words are commonly used. Of course, in the absence of snow and hail and severe frost, the chief characteristic of the winter is rain; hence some imagine that it rains much and often, but this is a mistake—winter days are generally clear and bright, and sufficiently cold to render them bracing. Fogs are unknown here. An Englishman on first landing discovers to his surprise that he cannot well judge of distance; his eye needs to be educated, the air is so clear that he imagines distant objects to be close at hand. In the North Island many flowers bloom all winter in the open air. A cottager there may often gather a more beautiful winter bouquet in his garden than many an English gentleman from his greenhouse. I had a *hedge* of choice geraniums round my garden the last year I was in New Zealand, and they flowered all winter. All English fruits flourish in New Zealand, and many rare and choice fruits are found there in great profusion. Two ripe crops of figs are often gathered in the same year, apricots, peaches, and grapes can be secured in abundance with little trouble. Hops grow well in the North Island. Oranges, lemons, and similar fruits grow and ripen in sunny spots, and with care, tobacco can be cultivated; but as yet labour is too scarce and dear in New Zealand to admit of extensive cultivation of tobacco or manufacture of wine. All the materials are there, in fact, for scores of profitable industries, lying undeveloped for want of people.

"' New Zealand is probably the healthiest country in the world. Its death-rate is about 12 per thousand—little more than half that of England; while its birth-rate is considerably larger. If it be answered that this is accounted for by the fact that only young people go there, the matter can be tested in another way. Dr. Thompson, who spent some years in New Zealand, and who wrote the very valuable work called *The Story of New Zealand*, tested the climate by comparing the health-tables of British troops in various parts of the world. No test could be fairer. He found that the death-rate per year per thousand was as follows:—Canada, 20; Malta, 18; Cape of Good Hope, 15; England, 14; New Zealand, 8. The deaths per thousand of *consumption* he found to be—England, 8; Canada, 6; New Zealand, 2.

"' On looking over the numerous colonies of the great and glorious Albion, and comparing them with New Zealand, it is at once evident that, of all the Colonial provinces of the British Crown, New Zealand bears the most resemblance to the mother country by virtue of its insular position, its climate, its soil, and the whole form and structure of the country. Blessed with a genial oceanic climate, so admirably suited to the Anglo-Saxon race, with a fertile soil, well watered and specially adapted to agriculture and farming; it is the country without dangerous animals, without poisonous plants, but rich in mineral treasures; a country where horses, cattle, and sheep thrive, where fruit, grain, and potatoes grow most abundantly; a country adorned with all the charms and beauties of grand natural scenery; a country which would easily support a population of twelve millions, and which promises the bold and persevering emigrant a lucrative and brilliant future. Such a country appears to be destined before all others to become the mother of all civilised nations.'

"A few hints, taken from the same source as the foregoing, as to the mode of procedure to be adopted by a new comer in New Zealand, will doubtless prove interesting here:—

"'Having selected his land, his first care is to build some sort of a house, which may be of logs or sawn timber. Sometimes the first erection is a "lean-to," the back part only of that which will one day be a permanent residence. If the new settler is a small capitalist, anxious to acquire a freehold property, he manages with very little furniture. A few stools, a deal table, a shakedown with blankets, and about £5 worth of crockery and cooking utensils, and the furnishing is, for the present, complete. Let it be noted here that life under such conditions, which would be unbearable in a climate like that of England, may be pleasant enough as a makeshift in a warm climate, where no one thinks it a hardship, and where it is accepted as on the high road to independence, and perhaps wealth. It is rarely wise to build and furnish a substantial house until this can be done from profits of the farm. To build the house and secure the first field of grass, fenced in, occupies the first year, and, when this is done, the preliminary troubles of a settler are over. His horses cost nothing to feed; he has dairy produce for his family and a few young stock.

"'No time should be lost in laying off land for garden and orchard and planting ornamental trees. Any labour spent in this way will be richly remunerative. This virgin soil, without manure, will readily yield from five to ten tons of potatoes. Carrots, weighing 8 lbs. to 10 lbs. each are very common, and other vegetables grow in proportion. Nothing will astonish the new arrival more than the rapid growth of trees and shrubs. I have seen pines 70 feet high and 11 feet in girth which have been planted within my recollection of New Zealand, *i.e.*, within fourteen years. Gum-trees can be grown from seed high enough for shelter in four or five years. Three years are enough to bring fruit-trees into good bearing. I saw on an estate lately, which four years ago was a dense swamp, an orchard with apple, peach, plum, cherry, and other trees in full bearing, and with grapes and raspberries, strawberries, &c., in almost bewildering profusion. From the same orchard the owner sold last year £100 worth of young trees raised from seed, besides planting out many thousands for his own use. Where trees grow so rapidly, there is a charm about planting unknown elsewhere, especially when planting on your own soil. This rapid growth is the effect of a warm, genial climate, where growth continues nearly the whole year round.

"'Having secured the first field, with the beginnings of garden and orchard, it now remains for the settler to bring the whole of his land into grass on farms where it is not already so, increasing his stock with his pastures. The next step will be to turn up his oldest grass-land and begin a rotation of crops. Fern-land will not generally give a good crop of corn until it has been long enough in grass to have become clear of the fern root and fibre; but it will yield very heavy root crops from the first. Comparatively few of the farmers in North New Zealand grow any crops for sale, preferring to confine themselves to grazing, which involves but little labour and pays well, bringing in a return of from £2 to £3 per acre per year; but I am satisfied that the English method of farming will pay best in the end, and that the plough must be kept going if justice is to be done to the soil.'

"'To encourage dairy farming in New Zealand, and to afford information to farmers in the outlying districts, the Government of New Zealand have appointed a gentleman of large experience in dairy farming in England to be Inspector of Dairies in the Colony, and Mr. William Bowron, who holds this appointment, in his valuable little work on the manufacture of cheese and butter in New Zealand, writes as follows:—

"'A gentleman in America reports the average yield of his cows at 680 gallons per annum. From that quantity of milk he produced 6 cwt. of cheese. I may remark that in England and America they can calculate upon grass for six months only; here in New Zealand we calculate upon grass for eight or nine months. My impression is that your cows during forty weeks will average not less than two gallons per day. I have stated this frequently in public meetings, and have been told that my estimate is below the mark. Two gallons per day is 560 per annum. Well, place the figures at 560, that quantity, at 4d. per gallon, will give the farmer, say, £9 for each cow.'

"'To say what New Zealand is capable of producing is impossible. Two acres and a-half will sustain a cow summer and winter; two and a-half million acres will keep one million cows; the produce of each cow would not be less than 5 cwt. of cheese, valued at 6½d., or £60 per ton, would produce a revenue of fifteen millions per annum, leaving out of our calculation the calf and also the pig which invariably goes with the cow.

"'Gold mines are good in their place, but at best uncertain, and are soon exhausted; but the green sward, when properly treated, never. Every spear of grass, from generation to generation, is tipped with gold for people who know how to utilise and extract it.'

"'For the information of all who may forward cheese to London, I may say that November, December, and January are the months when cheese is little sought after, and forced sales never pay. April, May, and June are the best months; the previous year's stock is all used up, and the cheese merchants are glad to take the first which comes to market. This fact presents a fine opportunity for New Zealand, as you will be able to send in thousands of tons of fine ripe cheese, just at the time when you will have no competitor. This I consider to be a point in favour of New Zealand. The same applies to frozen meat—avoid November and December. Shiploads of poultry, game, and rabbits come in from distant parts, depressing the meat market. There are also other causes which affect the meat market. Winter is setting in, trade is dull, and the large flock masters are killing off their draft ewes; all are sent to London, and the prices are unsatisfactory. Stretching over forty-five years, I never knew the market other than I have just stated. Butter realises the highest price in February and March; bacon in May, June, July, and August.'

"Cheese and butter factories have been established in the Colony with success. We insert an extract from the *New Zealand Herald*, of 29th April last. The Waikato correspondent of that paper (the leading journal of the North Island) writes as follows:—

"' Mr. Bowron, the Government Inspector of Cheese Factories, who leaves here to-morrow, takes down with him to Auckland a specimen cheese from each of the four local factories for testing and examination there. During his recent visit to Waikato, Mr. Bowron has visited each of the factories, and has expressed himself highly gratified with the successful manner in which the cheese factory movement has been firmly established in this district. Mr. Bowron recommends that the cheese should always, if possible, be shipped so as to reach home from February to May, that being the season of the year at which best prices will be secured. To the Rukuhia factory (that carried on in the old grand stand on the Ohaupo racecourse) Mr. Bowron gives the palm for superiority of quality. The cheeses are, however, small in size, which for the home market would be a disqualification, cheese of 90 lbs. weight being the favourite size. At Paterangi, Mr. Bowron was much pleased with the richness and quality of the cheese, particularly the "Cheddar," which he estimated would be worth in England from 70s. to 80s. per cwt. As a proof of the success of the Waikato Cheese Factory, it may be stated that though they have given 4d. per gallon for milk, a halfpenny more than the other factories, they will be able to declare a dividend of 8 per cent. for the season on the paid-up capital of the company.'

"The object of this pamphlet is to bring before the English public a few prominent facts connected with the colony of New Zealand, which render it so pre-eminently a desirable home for the English farmer, and an attractive place of residence for those who require a good climate. The Auckland Agricultural Company, Limited, have for sale in the Auckland district about 350,000 acres of good land, and they are about to subdivide and offer these lands for sale in England. The Estates are situated in the Waikato and Thames districts, and are within easy reach of the City of Auckland, from which they are distant about 70 to 100 miles by rail.

"Some portions of the land, in an unimproved condition, can be had at £1, 10s. per acre, and land sown with English grasses at from £3 to £6 per acre, according to position and state of cultivation.

"The Company will sell the land in large or small selections on terms of deferred payment, such as will suit any one, charging low rates of interest for two, three, or four years, and where it shall be proved to them that the purchaser has a sufficiency of capital to erect the necessary buildings and stock the land, the ordinary deposit will be dispensed with. In certain special cases also the Company will be prepared to let land on lease, with the option of purchase, but in these cases there will of course be restrictions as to cropping.

"The grazing lands of which these estates principally consist are well adapted for carrying both cattle and sheep.

"The unimproved and fern-lands, if simply burnt off, and grass-seed sown broadcast on the ashes, will very quickly make a fair pasture, but after the land has been under the plough, cultivated, and sown in the ordinary way with English grasses, a fine rich pasture with a good bottom can be obtained in two years.

"One of the most suitable styles of cropping for the arable lands on the estates has been found to be three years grass, one crop of corn, then one of turnips and back to grass again. Another good system is to have, say, one-third of the farm in pasture, one-third under the plough and the remainder under crop; root crops can be grown on these properties to great advantage. It has also been found that beet and tobacco can be grown in the North Island with much success.

"The Company's objects in selling may be summed up very shortly: The lands were bought years ago with a view to the cultivation and subsequent sale of same, very large amounts have been expended in improvements, drainage, &c., and the Directors are now of opinion that the estates are in a sufficiently forward condition to be put before the public for sale, the original intention being naturally that the Company should eventually make a profit out of their operations. The local demand for land in New Zealand, because of the smallness of the population, is not sufficient to absorb all the land now offered for sale, and it is thought that many English farmers will be glad to avail themselves of this opportunity for procuring a good homestead on easy terms.

"It is intended by the Proprietors to give full value to purchasers of their lands, it being their aim to so satisfy the latter that they may be in a position to recommend their friends to come and do likewise, and for this reason it has been decided to accept lower prices for these properties than was ever before contemplated, the Company looking to the increased value of the remaining portions of their estates, consequent upon the sale of and settlement upon the lots sold, to compensate them for the reduced prices at which they will offer these lands.

"The following additional information may be useful:—

"HOUSES.—The cost of erecting a four-roomed house suitable for a small family—with verandah—is about £150. A six-roomed house will cost about £250, and so on in proportion.

"FENCING.—An ordinary six-wire fencing with wood posts will cost from 12s. to 16s. per chain according to the situation and facilities for obtaining timber. The barbed wire fencing will cost about 2s. 6d. per chain extra.

"SHEEP may be purchased at from 5s. to 12s. each, according to breed, &c., and their wool may be calculated to realise about 5s. each per annum; besides which there is the already rapidly growing frozen meat trade which bids fair to do so much for New Zealand by relieving it of the surplus stocks of sheep, and by giving an immense impetus to the general prosperity of the Colony, and thereby materially increasing the value of all lands suitable for sheep runs.

"No work, whatever its size, dealing with New Zealand, would be complete without a more definite reference to this subject of Frozen Mutton, the export of which has now become one of the established industries of the country, and is of vital importance to its future welfare.

"In the South Island, where refrigerating chambers and stores are already in working order, the consequent reduction in the quantity of sheep has even now commenced to have its effect upon the value of same, and to increase the cost of land. In the North things are not in such a forward state; but efficient machinery is in course of erection, and erelong the power of this Island to also take its legitimate share in the export of frozen meat must have a similar effect upon both stock and land—an effect in which those now purchasing properties such as we are offering must participate. At present there have been difficulties in the way of the shipment of beef in a frozen condition; but there can be no doubt that a means of overcoming these will shortly be found which will again and still further enhance the value of property in New Zealand.

"The following figures will prove of interest in this connection, and will show the paramount importance of this trade to the Colony. The quantities of New Zealand meat received in England were as under:—

	Carcases of Mutton.	Quarters of Beef.	Number of Shipments.
1882, . . .	8,839	—	2
1883, . . .	120,893	728	15

"And it is already evident that the shipments for this year will reach 300,000 carcases.

"A competent authority on this matter has lately stated it as his opinion that New Zealand is at present capable of exporting from 400,000 to 500,000 carcases per annum, and that this quantity can easily be increased to a million within the next few years.

"CATTLE are obtainable as follows:—Milch cows at from £5 to £7 each; on some occasions, owing to depression in the markets, they may even be purchased for less money. Yearling beasts can be had at from 25s. to 45s. each, and two-year old beasts from 50s. to 90s.

"HORSES.—Good useful horses may be bought at from £10 to £15 each; and superior cart horses range from £20 to £30.

"Intending emigrants must give up the old idea that New Zealand is a long way off. In point of fact it is now only divided from England by a six weeks' voyage, owing to the direct lines of steamers which are now running between the two countries, and of which there are at least two per month. The steamers of the New Zealand Shipping

Company, Limited, load in the Royal Albert Dock (Gallion's Station), London, and the rates of passage-money to Auckland are as follows :—

	Each adult.
First class (saloon cabins), ...	60 to 70 gns.
Second class, ...	35 to 40 ,,
Third class (closed cabins with 2 berths) for married couples, ..	22 ,,
,, (,, 4 ,,), ...	20 ,,
,, (open berths, for men only), ...	18 ,,

Children under 12 years of age, travelling with their parents, half-price. Infants under 12 months, free. In the case of large families or parties coming from the same place and going in the same steamer, the Auckland Agricultural Company, Limited, can probably arrange to get a concession on these rates.

"Half the amount of passage-money is required to be paid on securing the passage, and the balance three days prior to the steamer leaving the docks.

"The following quantities of personal baggage—not merchandise or furniture—will be taken for each adult, free of charge, viz.:—Saloon, 40 cubic feet; second class, 20 cubic feet; third class, 15 cubic feet; any additional quantity will be charged for at the current rate.

"Packages for the cabin should not exceed 2 feet 6 inches long, 1 foot 6 inches broad, and 1 foot 2 inches high.

"For those preferring the greater length of a voyage per sailing-vessel the rates are as follows :—

Saloon cabin 43 guineas, with the use of bedding and cabin fittings.
    ,,   35 ,,   without   ,,   ,,
Second cabin 20 ,,
Third ,, 15 ,, (enclosed berths).
Steerage 13 ,, (open berths).

"The other regulations are as given above, but the sailing-vessels load in South West India and East India Docks here.

"As there are so many steamers leaving now, very few of the sailing-vessels take any but saloon and second-class passengers.

"Persons taking out money with them are advised to deposit the same with the Bank of New Zealand, 1 Queen Victoria Street, London, where they will get a draft, payable on demand in Auckland, for the sum so deposited.

"Mr. Samuel Grant, who went out to New Zealand some years back in conjunction with Mr. Forster as delegate from the Lincolnshire farmers, has just left by the steamer *Ionic* for Auckland with the view of inspecting the Company's properties, and on his return here in November next will be prepared to offer the same in lots suitable for persons with either large or small amounts of capital, and he will be in a position to impart full information of every kind with regard to such lands to intending emigrants and purchasers.

"In the foregoing it has been the endeavour to give information likely to be of service to those desirous of settling in New Zealand, and when comparison is made with other parts of the world to which emigration is from time to time directed, we think we may consider it proved that New Zealand offers the best field for those who wish to make new homes outside the mother country.

"LONDON, 26*th June*, 1884."

MILFORD SOUND.

Quietly, and very slowly, we glided onward, passing the Mitre, snow-clad and grim, in the early dawn (4.15), while right ahead the cold white face of Mount Kimberley, dotted here and there with patches of bush, passing slowly by the Stirling Falls, some 400 feet in height, falling into the basin a simple mass of foam. Some of the lower mountains are covered with green scrub to the water's edge. Nearly every mountain went sheer down into the deep blue water, so deep that anchorage is out of the question. In ten minutes we were quite surrounded by gigantic heights, and no outlet visible. Glaciers and snow fields of dazzling white rose from the wooded valleys. The basin or inner harbour is, I think, ten miles in circumference. The Bowen Fall is more than three times the height of Niagara, but the volume of water is small, and looks more like huge fans of spray. Hundreds of silver-like water-threads find their way to the lake. We landed in glorious sunlight, and for some hours employed our time in forcing a way into the tangled New Zealand bush. Huge tree ferns, red gum, supple jack, and a carpet of the most varied ferns and mosses possible to imagine, crowded together in wild profusion. This place has never been properly prospected. The only habitation is one hut, shared by an artist, a photographer, and a new arrival in the shape of a prospector. Of course, none will remain over a couple of months. Wild red honeysuckle, many varieties of veronica, and other gay flowers studded the green woods with colour. My photographs will give some idea of this beautiful spot. The sand-fly is very troublesome. Early Monday found us at the Bluff, thence by rail to Invercargill, 18 miles (Prince of Wales or Albion Hotel), a fairly large town with wonderfully wide streets and fine stone buildings.

LAKE WAKATIPU (OR STILL WATERS).

Next morning, 6.45, found us *en route* for Kingston, the head of Lake Wakatipu (leave out the u in pronouncing), after a slow journey of seven hours through long dreary flats, for the most part inhabited by rabbits.

In fact, we passed one station where the owner keeps between seventy or eighty hands constantly employed in doing nothing else but exterminating this great pest. The very last half-year they killed over 350,000 head (mostly by medicated grain), the total cost for the six months being £1,500, and the net return for sale of skins, &c., was only £780. Many farms that ten years ago were of great value are now practically useless, for sheep will not feed after these prolific little rodents. Until one sees and hears of the terrible destruction they cause, the foregoing figures seem quite impossible. Even the large hawk of the country is never shot; they may be seen in numbers wheeling over their furry prey.

After a grand sunny trip down the lake, surrounded by bold, bare mountains varying from 3,000 to 7,000 feet in height—many of the peaks covered in snow—we sighted the pretty little township of Queenstown lying at an angle of the lake. The weather all day had been simply perfect—a golden sunset left behind a peculiar shade of pink, shaded into palest gray. The place was full, owing to the Governor of New Zealand (Sir W. Jervois) being present. Our bedroom was a model for a barrack—four beds, four bare walls, and two of the most comical jugs I ever beheld. These jugs were originally made of ware, but age or disaster had gradually removed spouts, handles, and standing apparatus. These mishaps had been from time to time renewed by the local tinman, and what with a bandage of tin in one part, a spout of zinc in another, tin handles, and tin bottoms, they had indeed become china warriors; it is unnecessary to add that they leaked, and in the endeavour to pour water into the basin you generally found this useful fluid over your legs or boots. L—— was anxious to answer telegrams and letters, so St. John and I determined to do Ben Lomond. We started in company with Miss Godfrey, and a gallon of water, for the top. It was a cloudless summer day, very hot, not a breath of air. (All the foregoing has been written in great haste, and at a ricketty table, in order to catch mail, so please correct.) The first two hours of the ascent was a gradual rise of 3,000 feet over a rough stoney track, fairly trying to the feet, and occasionally when a wild Irishman put his long thorns into your homespun, trying to the temper also, hundreds of lizards glided away at our approach, and the ubiquitous rabbit scuttled into the scrub. Arrived at the Saddle, a grand panorama met the eye. Having very little time, we pushed on for the real work of the day, and with no path or guide we scrambled for two hours up the sides of this rugged old fellow (about 6,000), and finally rested on the second pinnacle from the top. Our lady was a splendid climber, and the way she pulled herself over boulders, tugged herself up by tussocks of snow-grass, was really wonderful. Time would not admit of our reaching the summit, as the boat for Kinlock-head started at five. This was hard, for another half an hour would have seen us there. After a rest, and a long, quiet look at the exquisite circle of snow-tipped peaks, embracing among others the Remarkables, and in the distance the bold white summit of Mount Earnslaw, we commenced the toe-breaking descent. I could not help admiring the sensible boots our little Sydney lady wore, and found to my surprise that she had just returned from England, and the said boots were made under her directions by a regular country shoemaker at Lynton (Devonshire). We scrambled back at our best pace, arrived at the hotel at 4.30, after seven and a-half hours' really trying walking, owing to the heat, but the half-hour's rest, with the view, well repaid the exertion.

EICHART'S HOTEL, QUEENSTOWN.

The summer evening's steam to Kinlock was particularly pleasant after our climb, and the grand scenery, with only here and there a saw-mill, gave an idea of solitude I have never experienced before—all quiet, except the skitter made by a brood of young ducks, or the flop of a huge trout as he engulphed some unwary grasshopper. Everything was so still that nature repeated itself in the dark blue water. In two hours Mount Earnslaw (9,000 feet) seemed to block the head of the lake. We were greeted at the little wooden pier by Mr. Bryant, who, with the help of his daughters, soon divided our party, and put us into three little wooden houses. My room was about the size of an ordinary dining-table—the bed, stuffed with snow-grass, and a first-cousin jug to that at Queenstown completed the furniture. We all supped together in a large wooden room, with a bright wood fire. Our fare consisted of a goose and rhubarb-pudding—this being partaken of at 9.30 necessitated a prolonged smoke, and as we looked over the primitive visitors' book we came across the names of

CHAS. JOHN TRIPP.
ELLEN S. TRIPP.
C. M. HOWARD TRIPP.
J. M.   ,,   ,,
E.   ,,   ,,
EDITH   ,,   ,,

} Cousins of Friends at Home.

When I tell you Kingston consists of three houses, and Kinlock-head of four, you may guess how grand the solitude. What I like is the primitive kindness of our hosts. I can assure you we gladly miss the English waiters crowding for the departing tip. We were up at five, and arrived at Invercargill at eight—very tired, and done up.

LETTER VI.

A LONG dreary ride from Invercargill to Dunedin. Both glad of a rest at Waine's Hotel, although, on a second visit, I should make The Grand my head-quarters. Being up at the Fernhill Club, we strolled round and found it a capital building, with a fine view and every comfort, the grounds being especially good. Dunedin (the Gaelic for Edinburgh) is a very handsome city of 40,000, principally Scotch. The buildings are *now* for the most part of stone, and high-class in point of architecture. Many of the private residences are built on the numerous surrounding hills, some reached by a wire-rope tramway—fast, safe, noiseless, and inexpensive. Dunedin must have a prosperous future. A farewell dinner with Mrs. B—— at the Grand, and Monday found us in the eight o'clock train for Christchurch, arriving after a weary journey of 12 hours; distance 230 miles, with *no less than* 75 stations *en route*. We passed over one bridge more than a mile long, the snow-water dividing the pebbly river-bed into numerous channels. Christchurch is the capital of the South, or rather Middle Island, and boasts a large cathedral, university, museum, banks, &c., all of fine stone, and a population of about 30,000. I met a gentleman at the C.C. Club who farmed 40,000 acres, and in one field alone he grew 2,900 acres of turnips. The Canterbury Plains are celebrated for rich soil and splendid breed of sheep, the best cross being Lincoln and Merino. I saw the wool from one animal just shorn, weighing in the grease 24 lbs.; animal weighed 110 lbs., and produced 40 lbs. of fat (or tallow), the growth of fleece being 11 months 14 days. The same squatter has one favourite field, producing last year 106 bushels to acre of wheat, and his general average is 60 to 70. The station farmers here are taken from some of the best blood in England. They are fine-looking, well-educated, and wonderfully well-read men, and most anxious to do everything for strangers. The Domain, or public park, is beautifully laid out; the river Avon winds slowly through the town. We stayed at the club, but Coker's Hotel is a useful place. We saw the skeleton of the celebrated wingless Moa bird, 14 feet in height (Dinornis maximus). The egg is larger than a man's skull. The kea is another native bird. This lively epicure fastens its long claws into the wool of the sheep, and the poor beast cannot shake him off. He eventually kills the sheep by driving a hole into the kidney, and that dainty bit is the only part he will touch. Christchurch and district has a real British look, and very little imagination would make you think yourself in England. The native woods are suitable for all kinds of work, but especially adapted for the cabinet-maker, and furniture veneers are very beautiful in texture and colour. The quantity and variety is simply incredible. The green Maori stone is about the only curio of these islands. The living is plain and good— beef and mutton from 4d. to 6d., excellent in quality and flavour; bread, cheese, and butter equal to any I know. Fish is scarce, but the celebrated frost fish is supposed to be an epicure's dish. The building stones are varied, striking in appearance, and easily worked. Lyttelton, the port of Christchurch, is a land-locked harbour, and the steamers of the New Zealand Shipping Company start from here. The *Aorangi* is a fine specimen of what an ocean-going steamer should be; in this age of cheap and universal travelling, each new steamer becomes an object of interest. The number of horses, and especially idle horses, is very noticeable; £20 will purchase a good animal, well-bred, fast, and sound. The wheat fields are usually from 50 to 200 acres, free from the pretty but noxious charlick. The hedges are nearly all gorse. The real Colonial is not a drinking man; it is the "new chum" or broken-down "old chum" who does the rowdy. For my part, I can hardly conceive a grander life than that of a pioneer in such a fine country as this. The man must throw up English ties—friends and the luxuries of an old civilisation—to reclaim by hard and incessant work the soil now given over to nature's gorgeous undergrowth, substituting for forest and plains of flax or nodding snow-grass the clover and more nutritious grasses of Europe. These hardy settlers reduce by their energy the cost of food, enabling the struggling masses in our densely-populated towns to live better and cheaper. The life is not a bed of roses, but it is a manly, healthy, contented life, and self-denial must be the motto for any successful man. What a real satisfaction it must be for a young fellow to see 50 sheep where one could only feed before. We went over a meat-freezing establishment, the *Aorangi* taking no less than 12,000 carcases of sheep in beautiful condition. The willow-trees here form a perfect cascade of waving green, sweeping the ground or water, having a most graceful look. Now for a very faint idea of our western drive from Christchurch on the east to Hokitiki on the west.

THE WESTERN DRIVE, OR OTIRA GORGE.

We left Christchurch and civilisation by the afternoon train; our little locomotive brought our party of six very slowly over a perfectly level landscape for 50 miles, with few charms except to the observant eye; but, when one sees nearly every field studded with sheep, horses, cattle, or nearly ripe corn, and then realises the fact, that 30 or 40 years ago the whole place was a howling wilderness, he can then feel proud of being an Englishman. For nearly four hours the little train jogged along at a snail's pace, stopping at small wooden stations (with seemingly no roads to or from anywhere), and then "toddled" on again and finally landed us at Springfield, a terminus at the base of blue-looking hills. To all appearances Springfield consists of about three houses and outbuildings, but doubtless, some half-dozen miles away, you might come across a home station or wooden shanty if diligently looked for. We had to *carry* our baggage, &c., to Cassiday's *Hotel;* and soon made ourselves very comfortable in a small room with a big fire. Our party consisted of Mrs. and Miss G——, Rev. Dr. D——, and our three selves. Cassiday, the proprietor, a driver for many years of the mail-coach (and now a small station-master and horse-jobber), beguiled the time by telling some wonderful escapes and accidents over this road, subject as it is to avalanches of stone—after rain many portions of the road slide clean away; these little tales were hardly reassuring, for *this year* the New Zealand rain-fall was much heavier than has been known for years. The pass was blocked two days ago, and one of the coaches overturned in a ford, nobody killed, but many of the mail-bags were lost. Very nice! This Western Road is said by men who have done America, Switzerland, and Norway, to be the finest drive in the world; and now that I have seen it, I can safely say it is most beautiful, and *scarey* to better heads than mine. I have read no description of this wonderful place, purposely to put down my own impressions; it is not so giddy as I expected, but for beauty and *marvellous solitude*, it is beyond anything I have ever dreamt of.

Were I an able man, I might place before you this Western Road; but it, like the writing, is full of irregularities and surprises. We got into our coach, and my first impression was rather a doubt as to its strength; but time proved it a splendid machine for the work. The team consisted of five strong useful animals, and our driver, "Maher," a capital whip. We were soon seated, rugs settled, and the small amount of baggage stowed. The driver gave one ringing crack of his long kangaroo skin whip, and away we went at a brisk trot. In less than a quarter of an hour we forded our first river, and although in no real danger whatever, the first sensation of being bumped over boulders of various sizes, from a lump as big as a bucket, to the small pebble, the horses splashing and slipping, but never really stumbling, was, to say the least of it, a novelty; young L—— and I had the back seat, and unless we had held on, nothing on earth would have prevented our being jerked into the water. The ascent of Porter's Pass is tedious, and rather nasty looking; the saddle, 3,240 feet, is anything but a comfortable place to look over, gradient 1 in 10. The view from the saddle is striking and wild, rather than beautiful, bare mountains and jagged peaks extending as far as the eye could reach, all still—no life whatever. On and on, leaving behind big masses of mountain, rich in every shade, from the deepest slate to the softest gray, patched with pale carmine; their snowy peaks glistening in the sunlight—the air pure, clear and bracing; trotting on between valleys of rocks encamped on the hill-sides like ruined cities or druid remains. About mid-day, we pulled up at the little "Accommodation House" of Craig-y-Burn; here the black birch relieves the somewhat monotonous landscape. A short distance from Craig-y-Burn, a very curious subsidence had recently taken place—sinking in the form of huge batteries, rising tier above tier, and giving one the idea of some continental city's outworks. Just before arriving at the Bealey, another striking effect opened up. Our road led us some 200 or 300 feet above a vast river-bed, probably from a mile to two miles in width, and bounded in the far distance by black mountains. The pebbly bed intersected by dozens of small, blue, snow-fed rivers, barkless trees lying stranded in every direction. How wild this must look in flood, goodness only knows. The view from the Bealey Pass is exceedingly beautiful, and a full moon added an indescribable charm to this lovely region. We rested the night at O'Malley's (The Bealey); two men sleeping in bedrooms not larger than good-sized packing cases. The beds were small, but quite large enough to contain lively neighbours beside the original occupants. Each little room has a joint-stock hair brush — anything but inviting — and tapu (sacred) to me.

I cannot pretend to describe in detail this glorious region. The impressions are clear enough to my *own* mind as pictures of mountains, lakes, waterfalls, river-beds, and dense forests, the latter looking in the distance like the finest moss instead of trees, so closely are they grown together. Our road wound over the pebbly flat we had seen the day before. An hour's terrible jolting carried us safely across more than a dozen small rivers, many deep enough to cover the pole; the five horses splashing, the driver cracking his whip or calling on his cattle, gave an animated effect to the picture. As we neared the gorge the scenery was of the wildest, and in one ford of the Waimakariri we were simply pulled by sheer force over the river, the recent rains having in places washed the ford away, substituting blocks of stone. I can assure you we clung like grim death to the trusty coach. Nearly all the rocks on the roadside were covered with pale gray lichen and the stones with red fungus, culminating into bright vermilion; this contrast to the many-shaded ferns beggars description. Instead of water, the grim mountains seem to send down huge cascades of shale and stone, looking in the distance like gray waterfalls. Arthur's Pass is simply one huge landslip, 5,000 feet high — in fact, about half a mountain has fallen, blocking the entire valley. The road winds gradually to the top, covered in places with flowers and tufts of white mountain daisies, these latter three inches across. From here the view is superb —2,000 feet above, the snow-tipped and glacier-seamed mountains; far down below, the thickly-wooded gorge, with foaming Otira gleaming like a thread in the sunlight. Soon after the zig-zag descent commenced. The road is rough and *rotten* in numberless places, crossed every now and again by little streams. At nearly every turn recent repairs were observable. The first part the driver made at a trot, and until we arrived at the cutting in the bare face of the cliff, we all stuck to the coach. At one bend the leaders were out of sight before the body of the machine turned the corner. It is needless to say this nasty bit was done by the horses at a walk. Young L—— and I were in the back, and we were literally over the precipice. After this we all walked, although there was no danger *here.* The look of the place was very unpleasant, to the ladies and myself in particular. *One mile* of this pass cost £20,000 to make. The workmen were slung over the mountain side by ropes, and virtually cut their way inch by inch into the solid rock, blasting being impossible, and finally finished the road by rivetting blocks of timber four feet over the gulf below, no rail or anything to protect one from falling. The cost of keeping the whole of this road in repair is over £10,000 a year (distance, 150 miles). At the bottom of the pass a long rest and homely meal awaited us, and we met a man who had just fished out a mail-bag lost two days ago. The remainder of this interesting and somewhat exciting drive took us through one of the most beautiful bits of New Zealand bush imaginable, and the road being in capital order, the relief from the previous jolting was priceless. Tall forest trees towering from 100 to 200 feet in height, black birch patched with bright *crimson mistletoe*, tree ferns, endless creepers, supple jacks, twisting everywhere; black pines, fuschia trees, the scarlet-blossomed rata, dead pines standing stark and white. Here and there some forest king had fallen, crushing into fantastic masses smaller brethren, his muddy matted roots, full of bright green ferns, the young fronds looking like burnished copper in the sunlight—thick mosses, ferns and flowers carpeting the whole. No human being has ever penetrated these dense and tangled forests, and nature runs riot. The remaining portion of the drive carried us through the "avenue" to Jackson's, and so finished the grandest sight I have ever witnessed, taken as a whole; no touts, no tourists, save ourselves—all solemn, quiet, primeval.

In this hard, *but not tiring*, drive of four days we must have forded forty rivers; and to give some small idea of the silence and solitude of this lovely country, we only passed two vehicles on the road—one being an old coach "stuck up" two years ago and left; the other, a waggon and team of six horses—also, one policeman on horseback, and four navvies. Maher, the driver, gave many bits of anecdote connected with this wild road. He told us—" In 1876, when the gold diggings were opened at Hokitiki, three extra coaches were used to convey the diggers, and once, when resting at some regular spot for lunch (in this instance, taken with them), the diggers seated on the rising banks around, the coaches in single file on the side of the pass, the horses in a shanty a little way off—suddenly a noise was heard, and somehow a river, that had been dammed out of its proper course for years, broke its boundary, and, sweeping down the hill-side, carried the three coaches and their contents clean into the gorge below; only bits of the fittings were ever found." The few Maories who live here are very rich, and last week one chief took unto himself a wife. Her trousseau consisted of three satin dresses—pink for the wedding; blue for the afternoon; and crimson for the ball in the evening. A very old Maori chief, being asked by the inspector for the Government about his title to the land he claimed, replied in a simple matter-of-fact way, that he had not only killed the previous owner, but that he had also eaten him. The word Maori means heart's blood.

These rough and unfinished sketches have been written under singular disadvantages — generally in a smoking-room, with flies buzzing, men chattering, doors opening, coming and going of every kind, bad pen and worse ink—but as down they are fairly faithful ideas of a grand, beautiful, and interesting country. At all events, they may give some idea of New Zealand to you at home. I may add, in conclusion, that one night, ten years ago, Jackson's house was swept clean away, and it was with the utmost difficulty the wife and children were taken to the woods on the back of an old mare. In the morning *acres* of land he had taken years to reclaim had vanished, and not a vestige of house or stables left, simply a new river-bed quite a mile wide. The floods here are sudden and terrible. Mount Cook, 13,200, is near this, and forms part of the range.

LETTER VII.

Drive to the Terraces.

LEFT Christchurch, or rather, Lyttleton, by the steamer *Rotomahana* for Wellington, fully expecting to see A. B——. It appears from later telegrams that my letters and telegrams must have missed. We found it impossible to wait, for upon consulting steamer and coach guides, we should have lost more than a week. Wellington is a busy, windy, and dusty place, suitable, no doubt, for business, but of little or no interest to the tourist. Steamer to Napier, a very curiously situated town, built on a strip of land hardly above the level of the ocean. Whilst here we witnessed a *grand sea*, the wind causing the rollers to dash ashore in a magnificent manner—the heaviest surf for thirty years. After spending three days at the Criterion Hotel, and seeing over Nelson's meat-works at Hastings, we left at six a.m. on Tuesday for the lake district. The style of conveyance same as used for the Otira Gorge, but travelling was by no means as comfortable, for we started with no less than eleven (including the driver, another really good whip)—one man seated on Jehu's knee, and a chum of the driver stretched on the luggage behind. A long drive over a sandy spit, in the keen morning air, brought us once more to the inevitable river, and with "a hang on, Charlie," to driver's friend on the luggage behind, and a crack of the whip, we rushed through the shallow water, sparkling in the sunlight. The day was bright and sunny, the atmosphere clear and bracing, clear, except in the distance, where a mist clung round the highest peaks. After many a breather—*i.e.*, a walk up the bad bits, and an occasional ford, we reached Pohui at 12.30, lunching off cold mutton, bread, and tea. A new, but to my mind a rather patchwork, team were now put in—a big white horse with lame fore-leg, a small white horse, and a cobby bay, as leaders, a mule and a small white mare took the pole—the wheels were carefully looked to and well oiled. An impressive drive of some dozen miles found us at Titiokura, the undulating upland extending as far as the eye could reach, broken up at frequent intervals by serrated ridges and globular boles. Vast tracts of bracken, extending for miles, here and there the whole mountain side black from recent burning, in the far distance thick clouds of smoke curling quietly upward from some bush-fire still at work; all around a *profound* silence. In stormy weather this place must be gloomy in the extreme, the sandy pumice road adding to the stillness, and heightening the effect. Every now and then our Jehu drew up at a road-side post-office, a simple pole driven into the soil with a wooden box nailed to the top; and now and then a shade more primitive still, a stick with a slit, and a letter stuck in the divided end; but no trace of human life, except a bridle path into the thick wood, and our own roughly-made track. Once we met a cavalcade of Maories, all on horseback, the ladies astride, each carrying (wrapped in a shawl) a pig, a baby, or a small dog. Now and then a dip—but in the main gradually ascending. About four o'clock we reached the highest point of the road, not far from the Block House (a spot where years ago a bloody fight with the natives had taken place), we commenced our descent. Tauranga Kuma is 2,200 feet high, and the steep side we had to descend exactly 1,250 feet in depth, the road itself covers no less than three and a-half miles, our real advance about half a mile. We rested a moment at the top, and I must admit the view and the general look of the track was not only impressive, but rather appalling; 1,200 feet below, a gorge, with dense forests on either side, the river Mokara running between like a silver streak, fearfully sharp turns of the rotten road visible here and there. Our driver was a consummate whip, driving with *knowledge* and ease. Off we started at a hand gallop, scattering the fine dust in every direction, whirling round corners with only a foot or so to spare, down and down at the same rapid pace, jolting and vibrating in the most alarming manner. A stumble, a broken trace, an unexpected bank of mud, and nothing on earth could have saved us from total destruction. Every now and then, when crossing a small rut made by a mountain stream, the coach rolled from side to side to a very uncomfortable degree. We were all thankful to find ourselves in safety on the level, having done the three and a-half miles in exactly sixteen minutes. Two places were pointed out from the bottom where coaches had gone over. The remainder of the drive was pretty, the golden pampas grass (tui tui), waving above the green bracken, and edging the river to Stony Creek, where the jolting as we crossed the ford was unusually bad. About six p.m., we reached Tarawera. Tarawera (burnt spear head) is a village of three or four houses. Mr. Brill did his best for us by way of rooms and grub — but my room hardly measured 10 feet square. Up at five and on for Lake Taupo. The earlier part of the drive was *very* beautiful, the air clear, everything fresh, the track gradually ascending through volcanic formations surrounded by dense bush (please always remember that here bush means a *mighty forest*, not a scrub, as we use the word in England); then over miles and miles of wearisome plateau — the road, or rather track composed of nothing but *white* pumice dust, the fine particles penetrating everywhere. Towards the close of a fearfully hot afternoon, Mount Reuapehu (9,100), and volcanic Tongariro (6,500), stood clearly out against a cloudless sky, the former covered with snow, the latter dark and solitary, sending into the still air a lazy wreath of white smoke. The whole drive was simply bone-aching, the last mile taken at top speed over a most atrocious set of ruts (mis-named a road), became simply unbearable; we struck our hats, heads, and backs against everybody and everything, the roof of the coach squashed in both L——'s and my bowler. We arrived at six, all looking the same uniform colour, literally smothered in drab dust, having done the 56 miles in 13 hours. After an unusually rough and tumble meal at the Lake Hotel, kept by a man called Gallagher, who dispenses very poor and dirty entertainment, seasoned with rough and uncouth manners, and the study of economy in the way of politeness must be his custom. We visited after dinner, so-called by courtesy, (for it was an atrocious meal), a Geyser about two miles from the Hotel, and were well rewarded by seeing three fine volumes of water, some 40 feet in height; the moonlight added to the effect, and I can assure you it was very uncanny picking our way without any path through the scrub, with the steam wafting here and there, coming up from unexpected quarters, the river flowing below, and the noise of the bubbling water close at hand. On our return we were very much taken with the beautiful appearance of Lake Taupo, black Tongariro, and white Reuapehu, looking very lovely in the moonlight. The hotel was crowded, so I very reluctantly allowed another man and perfect stranger to sleep in the same room with myself. My gentleman did not trouble to undress, and *less* than two minutes completed his morning toilet. Our next day's drive was full of incident. We started with a new driver, a wretched team, and a tumble-down coach—before we had covered ten miles, the coach came to grief, and had it not been for a Mr. Bold (electrician to the Government, and constructor of the very road we had been travelling on for days), we might have been seriously delayed. He utilised some telegraph wire, odd rope, &c.—we then set out again. A few miles further, and a very much more complicated fracture occurred. By the merest chance we were only a mile or so from a log shanty, and after some delay in cutting down a sapling, strapping the same to the remaining bits, we once more took to the track, the poor old bandaged concern in the most sorry condition. It was a laughable sight to see the passengers holding up the body of the coach, while our best man, Mr. Bold, did the necessary repairs, quietly seated on the ground beneath the body of the wretched thing.

The heat was great, not a drop of water to drink, and we, being very thirsty, even finished up the remains of a "Billy" containing cold tea. The road so-called was simply a well-worn track over pulverised pumice stone, glittering with powdered fell-spar—the fine dust found its way everywhere. We lunched off mouldy sardines, apricot jam, and tea. This luxurious meal over, we seated ourselves beside the beautiful Wiakato, and smoked a pipe in comfort, for the jolting made a smoke in the coach dangerous to the lips. The last mile or so before reaching Ohinemutu was most refreshing—a delicious breeze wafting the odour from a regular *jungle* of sweet briar. We met a few of the *Carthage* passengers (C—— P——, &c.) at the Lake Hotel, Ohinemutu, and spent a pleasant hour or so chatting over experiences. Next day we all bathed together in the "Priest Bath," a sulphur pool. It was a funny sight to see the seven brown heads just peeping out of the milky-looking water. This water has the power of turning the body a beautiful red. "Madame Rachel Bath" has also a peculiar effect on the skin, and no end of ladies go in for it. The whole of the ground in this district is covered more or less with fire-holes bubbling, steaming, simmering, and hissing—a grand place for pigs; we saw one fine old fellow lying in a warm mud bath, grunting deep satisfaction as the sun streamed down on the unboiled part, baking and boiling his fat carcase at one and the same time. This is near the Maori district (King Country), and we saw many a fine specimen of the native race; they are all very fond of rum. One dusky beauty looked very striking, attired in a *bright* red petticoat, bust arranged à la Josephine, black tangled hair, two wisps of curls, like celery tips, plastered at the sides of her forehead, smoking a black clay pipe. This good lady had been worshipping Bacchus, and drunk would feebly express her condition. I am sorry to say spirits have a great fascination for all these natives, and they gradually barter land and everything for it. For the most part they are bright and happy, very strong, and with the most expressive eyes I have ever seen, easy in their bearing, and I soon got to like them very much. Dozens of bronze children, perfect little models, dive for pence in Lake Rotorua, and swim like seals soon after *two* years of age. We strolled into the Ranunga or Palaver House, and I noticed some thirty natives quietly circled around, their faces (some only tatooed) simple, earnest, grave, listening with attention to an address in Maori on the new plan for the township of Ohinemutu. These singular people have many types, some of the men and women strikingly handsome, with noble features, aquiline noses, and strong, tall, muscular frames; they all possess a very nice manner. It is rather wierd to go out alone at night, and in *perfect* quiet listen to the bubbling, seething, and steaming of this singular place, to feel and smell the sulphur vapour, and then imagine that the whole crust might easily give way.

THE TERRACES.

The drive between Ohinemutu and Wairoa is one of the prettiest imaginable; it passes through the Tikitapu Bush for about a mile, grand trees in one continuous stretch. The Remu pine, with its drooping spines, being very numerous, many trees hung with lichen, looking like hoary Titans, or perhaps coiled in the arms of the dark-stemmed supple Jack. Rocks lie scattered here and there, arched over with ferns whose fronds measure ten or twelve feet in length. This deep dark bush of New Zealand is green *all* the year round.

Coming out of the Forest, the beautiful Lake Tikitapu or Blue Lake bursts into view. Passing over a gentle rise, we come to the Green Lake, literally fringed with fern. The mirror in these deep basins is sometimes so perfect that one can hardly judge where reflection commences. These lakes take their names from the colour of their water. We slept very comfortably at MacRae's Hotel, and early next morning a short walk brought us to the native Boat-house on the border of Lake Tarawera. Six lusty Maories soon pulled us to a whare (native hut made of rushes), where we purchased a basket of *live* cray fish, and much to our disgust our oarsmen ate some of them alive, shells and all. These fish are about the size of a very large prawn, and are truly delicious. A further pull of five miles (making nine in all) finished the trip to Rotomahana. After a dusty walk of a mile, the famous White Terrace came into sight, and I must confess to a sense of disappointment with its first appearance. Having put on cheap slippers bought for the purpose, we commenced climbing up the delicate steps of this marvellous place. You may paint and photograph, but never give any idea except that of outline. Each terraced edge, composed of numberless little basins full to the brim of clear water, dripping slowly to the ledge below, forming in the course of years myriads of tiny stalactites—all of pure white silica. The pools take every shade of blue. These coral-like formations can only be *"wondered at"*—not described. The White Terrace is about 100 feet high, and the lowest step is some 200 yards wide, graduating to the top, from whence the supply of boiling water comes. Sometimes this huge cauldron at the summit takes the form of a low but powerful geyser, sending volumes of water in a big rush over the fairy terrace; each step, or *part of a step*, takes the crescent form. Try and imagine the whole of this natural formation to be fine *white* petrified moss, and that may perhaps help you to the picture. Terrace after terrace, tinted pool after tinted pool. Every here and there sulphur has fringed the lips of these dainty cups with bright golden hues. A lazy cloud of steam gives a peculiarly sensuous feeling to the whole.

After leaving the White Terrace we came to a great boiling well, which is intermittent, sending up great volumes of water every few minutes to the height of 10 or 15 feet—the Devil's Hole, hooting with a blast like a hundred steam engines; the bright still COPPER green lake. The porridge-pot is a moving mass of hot Fuller's earth, rising and falling with the pressure from below; the natives eat this, but we found it scarcely good value. During our examination of the White Terraces the guides had cooked our cray fish (koura) in a boiling spring, also potatoes, and I would give anything for an artistic sketch of our luncheon party. We sat on stones, or bunches of dry grass by the margin of the lake, two canoes drawn up alongside with a bright-eyed Maori child in the bows of the nearer. Kate, our guide, a native policeman (who, by-the-bye, was a Maori woman) sharing the cray fish with us. A very old tattooed Maori (who owned to a great liking for human flesh) and a couple of younger men shelled the fish and helped us through our simple meal. It was a quaint picnic — 5

Englishmen, 2 Maori women, 3 Maori men, and the bright-eyed child—the bubbling of steam-holes the only sound, the pretty long-legged sand-pipers the only audience. On first acquaintance, the canoe did not convey a deep sense of security, but custom soon made us feel at home squatted on our hams in the bottom of this hollowed old tree; every now and then she took in a little water over her ricketty bulwarks. Arrived at the other side we landed on the Pink Terrace. This terrace is not so high as the white, nor so broad, but each step is more clearly defined, and in my humble opinion is much the prettier of the two. Hang the snobs!!! was our exclamation on seeing the pencilled names in every direction over this beautiful work of nature. "Who cares for Brown, Jones, and Robinson! Who wants to know that one is an auctioneer and another an ironmonger," &c.! Cads like these have, in this case, gained a very cheap immortality, for by the action of the chemicals in the water a deposit becomes glazed over the pencilled names and thereby made for ever indelible. As I said before, I do not intend to describe the hundred beauties of these unique terraces—the soft pink steps of every shade; now and then pale sulphur tints would mingle with the pink and fade into palest gray; the bright cobalt blue basin at the top, with its yellow bank graduating to pink at the edge, forming a most perfectly even tracery of pink moss; a long, long bath in these beautiful, warm, blue pools; the dark-skinned natives showing in contrast to the delicate colours around, and as we all stood round the basin leaning on the edge of our natural bath the effect of colour was very striking.

We now all got into one canoe, recrossed Rotomahana, and glided pleasantly down Kaiwaka's rapid stream, the banks fringed with tall green rushes, dotted here and there with wild convolvulus; still the same quiet uninhabited feelings — a wild duck flushing, the only sound. Another pleasant pull of an hour and a-half, beguiled by Maori and English songs, brought us once more to Wairoa, all having spent a day that will afford conversation for years to come.

27th Feb.—We are now saying good-bye to New Zealand, and in an hour more shall be on our way to Sydney by the *Ringarooma*. I can safely say I leave this country with deep regret. The climate, the soil, the grand foliage, the mountain ranges through which we have worked have afforded plenty of pleasure for eye and mind. This country must have a fine future. I cannot say our 500 miles of coaching has been all comfort, but now the memories of quaint picnics, hard seats, and little mishaps are pleasures, not drawbacks. We drove to Cambridge and thence by rail to Auckland. From Mount Eden the view of Auckland and the two splendid harbours is most charming. We took steamer to Wiawera Hot Springs, and enjoyed a quiet Sunday at this prettily situated watering-place. Miss Graham did the honours of the house, and made us more than comfortable.

LETTER VIII.

SYDNEY, BLUE MOUNTAINS, &c.

12th March.—We both felt great regret at leaving New Zealand, with its southern Alps so rich in grand scenery, and its daily life teeming with incident. By-the-bye, that reminds me of the Otira Gorge; we met a young doctor who did the drive a few days after us, the coach was upset in crossing a ford, a little girl with himself nearly drowned, the whole coach fell over; of course the passengers on the waterside lay struggling for some time, but all escaped with a nasty ducking. It is difficult to describe things in the hurry and rush of travel, but the memories of the Sulphur Springs rising and falling with mystic sounds on the desolate plains of Ohinemutu, the perfume of the bush fires floating on the quiet summer air, reminding us as they did of some Italian cathedral thick with incense. The evergreen forests carpeted with princely todeas, the mellow note of tui tui (parson bird), the clear, balmy air, the musical language of the Maories, will, I trust, remain as pleasant thoughts for years to come. The pakehah (Maori for stranger), was pleased!! The Colonials themselves are, in nearly all classes except the very best people, especially untidy, and careless of the refinements of life. Clubs, with a large number of beds are a necessity, for many, if not most, of the hotels are rowdy, dirty, and the joint-stock hair-brush plainly shows the general habits of travellers; the grub is badly cooked and often tough, the only *really* tender mutton I remember tasting in New Zealand had been to England and back in a frozen condition, that was simply delicious, and we thoroughly appreciated our lunch at the Wellington Club. The voyage in the *Ringarooma* from Auckland was unpleasant, the ship dirty, and frequently the meat came to table unfit for food. On Monday, the 3rd March, we steamed into Sydney harbour. This magnificent harbour is broken up into charming bays, wooded to the water's edge, and in most places the shore line is deep enough to berth the biggest ship afloat. Port Jackson Heads may be a quarter of mile wide, but the whole of Sydney harbour has a water boundary of 1,400 miles. Pretty villas and long verandahed houses are dotted here and there. Soon the bays looked larger, the houses more closely packed, and Sydney, with its crowd of shipping, busy wharves, countless ferry steamers, lay before us, situated in the most pleasing and picturesque position possible to imagine. Petty's Hotel is very comfortable for a Colonial hotel, but for rough feeding, bad waiting, recommend me to the general run of hotels in the Colonies; they are for the most part managed or owned by the Irish. Dirt, flies, tumble-down sofas, soiled table-cloths, hat-stands guiltless of pegs, doubtful chairs, and the windows, if by chance you can open them, are sure to run down with a bang when least wanted to do so. The bedrooms are in *all* cases small, generally innocent of paper, and often divided by a simple wooden partition; this latter element makes a lively neighbour anything but an agreeable companion—up to the present

I must surely have enjoyed a greater variety of nasal music than falls to the lot of ordinary mortals. Sydney is a well-built but irregular town of 270,000. It can fairly boast of good but rather narrow streets. Some of the buildings are very fine, notably the post-office, although at present the façade is spoilt by a conceit of the architect, who, being anxious to hand down to posterity the exact style and costume of 1880, has given to the world a most grotesque series of carvings—on one panel you will see the modern postman, another panel portrays the betting-man, the next, perhaps, the girl of the period, the following the shopman, with frock coat and Dundreary whiskers, likely enough its fellow will be the judge in wig and robe, again the masher, then perhaps the corn stalk (or young bushman); in short a more horrid, and *badly executed* design I never beheld. I fancy the Government intend removing these monstrosities, at least I hope so. "Doing the block" is about the daily routine, *i.e.*, strolling quietly up George Street, down King Street, along Pitt Street, and up Hunter Street; here you meet everybody from 11.30 to 12.30, or 3.30 to 5. The Colonial girls have good figures, and, in the season, generally dress in nice clean white or light dresses, and nearly all have a regular cockney accent.

The telegraph boys in scarlet jackets, riding at a gallop here, there, and everywhere, make a novel and striking picture. The larrakin (or rowdy) is bred in, and, thank goodness, confined to, the Colonies; he is a voter, always a red-hot Radical, with a bitter hatred of the "educated and refined," always anxious to vent his spleen on anybody or anything respectable. You can see hundreds of these young ruffians about, all dressed alike in the soft felt billy-cock hat, shirt innocent of collar, hands in pockets, pipe in mouth, leaning against the walls, doorways, and verandah pillars of public-houses. They are slouching and sly, generally possessing the happy knack of kicking old women to death, or assaulting little children. Manhood suffrage prevails here, in the lower classes it breeds a more than independent spirit; a great body, of which the mechanic, waiter, shopman, small store-keeper, domestic, porters, guards, and stewards form a part, have sadly misconstrued the meaning of the word independence, substituting a rough-and-ready insolence of manner, at once useless, quite unnecessary, and particularly distasteful. As a rule, men are poor because they are indolent, or out of health, but no wild doctrine of an equal division of wages or money will mend the matter. I may add the pale, "mealy-faced" larrakins are always running down Old England, and are of the class who would use dynamite without hesitation. We went by train over the Blue Mountains to Mount Victoria, a gradual rise of 3,422 feet, the line a splendid bit of work. Drove from the Imperial Hotel to Govett's Leap, once again the coach " stuck up," but after some delay, and a considerable amount of bandaging, we proceeded on our journey; again I may safely say there is no monotony about coach travelling in the Colonies. Shortly after our breakdown we sighted a huge canyon, extending for miles and miles, over 3,000 feet below, covered with what the driver told us was blue gum, but this forest may have been closely packed bushes for ought I could make out to the contrary. It takes over four hours to ascend the 3,400 feet, and yet you can lie over the edge of the awful place and drop a stone clean down to the bottom of this terrible gorge without touching anything on its way. No man has ever been known to have entered this enormous basin except Govett, the bushranger, who jumped over to avoid the police, hence "Govett's Leap." From Mount Victoria you can see for fifty miles over undulating ridges cut up into deep canyons, covered with nothing but gum trees, of which there are over 200 different sorts in Australia. The Zigzag Railway is a marvellous work of engineering skill, working down from 3,658 feet with a backward and forward movement. L—— and I went down in the guard's van of a mineral train; as you go down one level you may see the line again on the level below. I returned to Katoomba (Great Western Hotel). Spent a very pleasant evening with the North family. Next day we rode through the bush to the Katoomba Falls, Orphan Rock, Fern Gully, Katoomba Colliery, and other places of interest. The name Blue Mountain is taken from the peculiar appearance these mountains have from a distance. Returning from a long drive the blue effect was on one occasion *very marked*, the distant peaks glistened in the setting sun like bright blue steel, the long white arms of the gum trees made natural frames, clearly marking this deep blue colour, not a leaf moving, the half-stripped branches of the trees stretched forth in gaunt effect, the evening calm and silent.

LETTER IX.

THE HAWKESBURY RIVER.

HAVING heard so much about the fine scenery connected with this beautiful river, I made up my mind to go, with a party if possible, if not by myself. A travelling friend of ours, called S——, stumbled across an advertisement, stating that the "Ocean-going steamer, *Admiral*," would start from Circular Quay at 9.45, for a trip up the Hawkesbury River and back, so L——, H——, S——, and I arrived at the wharf in good time, and found the ocean-going steamer to be nothing more or less than a tug-boat. L—— was for turning back, but I, being anxious not to miss the excursion, declined, and finally he kindly waived the chance of discomfort—and all started. During the night the wind had been getting up, and even inside the Heads the white-crested miniature rollers looked angry; but, once outside, the sea was very bad indeed (even to us old seafarers), and the captain should at once have turned back—but even at that early period of the day I detected some slight signs of drinking, so out of sheer bravado he kept on. Our fellow-passengers consisted of some half-dozen females, and perhaps double the number of men—

I may safely say we four were the only people on board with the slightest title to the term gentleman. A fat jolly publican's wife and her barmaid sat in the stern, quietly receiving the spray as it flew across the deck, rather enjoying it than otherwise; the rest of the passengers. bar ourselves, were soon anything but comfortable. The wind was due south, and with us, so after a *fast*, but really nasty passage, we steamed into the Hawkesbury River. For miles it is very like what Sydney Harbour must have been before the town itself was built; the river, or rather estuary wound in and out through mountainous scenery, the water taking the form of a series of lakes, wooded with green to the very edge, and had it been less cold and dull, no doubt we should have appreciated its beauties. We landed and dined in a corrugated iron shanty, with about a dozen or more big, leather-belted men, navvies I think; some clad simply in trousers, shirts, and soft felt hats, others better dressed, but these latter were all from the "larrakin class;" the whole meal was rough and rushed. After a short stroll we again got on board the *Admiral*, with the addition of some dozen or so taken from our dinner mates. We were interested in the scenery, until we made Broken Point, and once again found ourselves fairly in the open sea. During our trip up and down the Hawkesbury, the wind had increased to a "southerly buster." This playful gentleman was now lashing the water into fury, our little steamer being dashed into every position by the huge seas, and from her deck the waves looked immense. The leaden waste of sky, wild winds, and tumbling clouds appeared anything but comforting, a fellow tug turned back, making for shelter, but our captain in pure devilment kept on. The sea and foam began to dash over her, L—— made for the engine-room; we three laid hold of the iron bar where the big hook for towing is fixed, got a coil or so of rope to stand upon, and simply waited. Nobody could stand without holding on, and all were drenched to the skin.

The spirit bar was somewhat sheltered, and therefore getatable, and soon a number of larrakins were drunk; some lying on the deck, others holding on to *anybody* or anything. The chief engineer was encouraged to drink by a sturdy brute in a fur cap; the only two sailors on board were fast becoming drunk and incapable. The captain now saw danger, and pulling himself together, tried to get the bar closed, but to no purpose, and finding the sailor was steering so badly he was obliged to take the wheel, upon which these wretches stormed, or perhaps I should say held, the bar, and *free* drinking was the result. We expostulated, but of course to no purpose. It was a horrid sight. *Raw brandy* out of tumblers soon finished the men only half gone before. We could not keep the engineer to his room. He was up and at the bar every few minutes; once he fell slap into the engine-room. One frightful dip, and away floated part of the bulwark on the port side; next lurch, the clock and steam-gauge (as I found from L—— after) came to smash, and very soon the stoke-hole was some inches deep in water. Another terrific lurch, and a piece of timber fell on the legs of a big larrakin, bruising them very severely, and about half a dozen iron bars got loose, rolling from side to side in a somewhat nasty manner. This tug had no real cabin, but a sail-room forward. Into this the women and children were dragged or pushed, and the sky-light closed down, and for two hours we went at half speed in the teeth of a very heavy and dangerous sea; the rain came down. What with the foam and constant rush of water on the deck, everybody and everything looked bad. A dozen or more were lying about horribly sick; nobody could possibly stand over the side, as the bulwarks were so low. The storm continued with greater force than ever. We appeared to be making little, or very little way, and nothing could have looked worse.

We three were still holding on to the bar, red-eyed and stupid, when, amid the howling of the wind, the rattling of the engines, we heard screaming and shouting forward, and found the sky-light lifted clean off, with no end of water in the hold. After much trouble, it was patched up and tied down.

The little steamer behaved splendidly, and at last seemed to be gaining headway. It was close on night when we steamed through Sydney Heads, in company with the *City of Grafton*, a paddle-steamer of over 500 tons, and when I tell you we could now and then see from her bows to her paddle-wheels clear of water, you may imagine what the sea was like. What a terrible risk our little craft (75 tons) had escaped none can tell. Had the engines given way, or one green sea got into the engine-room, nothing could have saved the boat. Moral—This is the way to spend a happy Sunday!!!!

LETTER X.

BRISBANE, WARWICK, GLENELG.

I STARTED on the 18th March for Brisbane by the *Maranoa* (Queensland Shipping Company), a very comfortable steamer of 2000 tons. The day was perfect, and Sydney Harbour, lying beneath a cloudless sky, covered with a mosquito fleet of white-sailed yachts, looked simply lovely. Some local Regatta being on, the whole Harbour, and Rose Bay especially, appeared literally alive with craft of all kinds. The forty-eight hours' steaming along the coast was a pleasant run for those on deck, but made in awfully hot weather.

My cabin companions were simply nasty to a degree—drunk, incapable, and sick the whole voyage. It is difficult for a man quite unused to wield the pen to write the story of his travels without wearying his readers, and doubtless my similes have been repeated over and over again, but I really cannot help it. Moreton Bay is a large shallow lagoon, nearly surrounded by land, buoyed out for the traffic. The Brisbane River itself is broad and circuitous, banked by low-lying marshy soil, and just now rich in bright green maize. The Chief Justice of Queensland was a passenger on board the *Maranoa*, and in honour of his return a steamer decked out with bunting awaited our arrival, and the old gentleman (Sir Charles Lilley) received a very warm welcome from his friends of the bar. Brisbane itself is a new and well-built city of some 20,000. As usual, the public buildings are magnificent. The new Queensland Club, overlooking the Botanical Gardens, and close to a small lake covered with *huge* golden-shaded water-lilies would put to shame many of the largest Clubs in the old country. The Original Club-House is a quaint old place—the dining-rooms, &c., in front, the bedrooms arranged, at the back on three sides of a quadrangle overlooking a garden full of tropical flowers, the beaugain villia and yellow alamanda trailing all over the roof; every bedroom on the ground-floor opens out on this creeper-covered verandah.

At seven o'clock on any morning you might safely count upon seeing a dozen pyjamed men leaning on the balcony, sponge in hand, towel on arm, chatting, and waiting their turn for the all-glorious tub, the hot sun pouring down, making a return from the morning's shower "too awfully nice," and about the finest time in the day for a quiet cigarette.

E. B—— met me at the Club, and an introduction followed to some good fellows. The evenings spent at Neustead with the H—— family (Queensland merchant) will remain a pleasant reminiscence. Neustead is situated on a spur of the Brisbane river, high enough up to catch all the breeze, but near enough to see the passing and repassing of steamers, yachts, canoes, &c. The building is a *very* large one. Every room opens out on a huge verandah, the latter quite surrounding the entire premises, fitted with dozens of lounge chairs, afternoon tea tables, sofas, hammocks, small trees in pots, china sets, &c. Neustead is *quite* an open house, and Mrs. G—— H—— a charming woman with married children, but wonderfully full of life and good-nature, untiring in fun; she leaves on the 10th for England on a visit to a married daughter. On the same afternoon you may see some twenty people chattering and laughing— the daughter with her friends, the son with his chums, old H—— with his cronies, and so on—no stiffness or humbug, go or come, do what you like. They often hold scratch dances on moonlight nights, and the whole suite of rooms—dining, drawing, reading, and smoking—open with French windows from ONE side of this jolly old house. They have lived twenty years under the same roof, and Neustead is another name for hospitality.

During the day I felt the damp muggy heat of Brisbane to be very bad, sometimes the heat has been 120 in the shade, but during my short stay I was more fortunate, although the dull glare was far too much for my somewhat delicate eyes. After spending two or three days here, B—— and I started for the Bush. We spent one evening at Warwick with the D——'s, a small family of some dozen or so, and early next morning a light American buggy and two well-bred chestnuts soon put the township far behind. The whole country round here, and, in fact, everywhere is suffering from *severe* drought, no vegetation whatever, everything looking parched and dry to a degree quite unthought of by you at home; the barest cricket patch on Durdham Downs would be rich in grass compared to the Darling Downs just now. We called upon old Jacob Kercher, a Queensland wine grower—went over the vineyard, into his cool cellars, and as the carbonic acid gas escaped the mystic bubblings were very audible. The old chap was originally a practical man in a German vineyard, settling here 20 odd years ago, now his little property is a very valuable possession—old Jacob makes pure and good wines from the best stock in Europe. We sampled Hermitage and Hock and went on our way rejoicing, leaving an order with the old gentleman, that, I trust, may help to make some of my readers as jolly as it made us. A drive through an Australian bush is novel but monotonous. Everywhere the *everlasting* eucalyptus, growing at a distance of some ten yards or so apart. On and on over the dry hard land—all silence and solitude. About mid-day we reached a creek—there the horses were watered and fed, ourselves also taken care of. Soon the country looked better, and I found we were going through Glenelg. Later on in the afternoon we passed nine-mile gate. Shortly after M—— and H—— cantered up to meet us. M—— on Rocket, a dark well-bred chestnut, M—— looking very bright and really little altered, perhaps a trifle stouter. The welcome was hearty. H—— appeared much the same, if anything, a shade thinner, but the bush has evidently given him self-confidence, and he looks altogether tanned and wirey. During a rainy season, Glenelg must be very pretty; the house is situated on rising ground backed by a hill, the cluster of buildings covering a large extent, and surrounded by the not to be too much-prized verandah, covered with vines and a grand Westeria, the latter with a stem as large as a man's leg, shading by itself the supports and roof over one side of the house. The wool shed, out-buildings, store, and cottages form a somewhat imposing group all on the banks of a creek, just now rather dry. I am told some of the water holes contain rock cod 10 to 40 lbs. in weight. I saw one 4 pounds. The children met us at the bottom of the hill, anxious to see what the new Uncle H—— was like. B—— the elder was soon hard at work unpacking a new saddle his father had brought home for him, and the others showed their good taste by deserting uncle for sweets, toys, and beads. They are nice-looking, well-grown children, with beautiful eyes and eyelashes—the baby a splendid specimen. B——'s station is 245 square miles in extent, and in a good season he must do well. The garden at the foot of the hill and close to the creek is nicely kept by "John Chinaman." The house garden is round the house planted with roses, &c., but just now dry and unlovely. I went out kangaroo shooting one day, and although I saw a lot, did not get near enough for a shot. A long ride through the Australian bush is novel. Yesterday we had a fishing picnic, and my start was anything but amusing. B—— had a new horse called Charcoal, one I had ridden quietly enough before, and B—— has frequently been on his back. This time I was hardly on when he gave a terrific buck, pitching me clear up into the air; thank goodness I landed on the part nature intended for accidents of a similar kind, a big bruise and a nasty shaking the only result. A buck-jumper puts his head between his legs, brings all four legs together, makes one bound into the air, arching his back into a half-circle. Seeing I was all right, we all laughed, and I laughed, but I can't say much for the heartiness of my attempt—I fancy a grin would better express my meaning. Charcoal left the company, and spent the day in the bush. There are traces of gold all over Glenelg, and after seeing the ladies, H——, and M——'s eldest boy safe under the trees by the side of the creek, we drove to the diggings, but, owing to shortness of water, no work was on. E—— B—— gave me two capital specimens of gold in the quartz. The heat is VERY GREAT, the sky hard and brazen, the country perfectly dry, and unless rain comes shortly the suffering and loss must be TERRIBLE. The kangaroo does well here, and during the last three years 16,000 have been killed on this station alone. The flies are simply lively beyond expression, as for writing, reading, or sleeping in peace, it can't be done. All M——'s children have active and industrious feet, and as they scamper round the hollow wooden-floored verandah they make a noise calculated to upset a saint, much less a man stiff and sore from yesterday's fall. The laughing jackass, or settler's clock, and I are well acquainted; he commences his demoniacal row at sunrise and sunset. B—— looks at home as a squatter, dressed in white, with broad-brimmed straw hat, and dark tanned face. We ride everywhere—unless on horseback you may safely say we are seated or lying at length under the shingle-covered roof of the verandah. No carpets in the house, simply beautifully clean boards, with furs, rugs, &c., lying all over the place. I leave here in about a week for Sydney, and shall not be at all sorry to see San Francisco, for steamers with huge smoke stacks, staring dead lights, stuffy cabins, are becoming a trifle tedious. I suppose my next letter will be posted from 'Frisco, or I may get a chance for a line or so at Sydney. I think the most curious thing in the whole of these flourishing Colonies is the astounding fact that rents should be double what they are in the crowded and circumscribed towns of England. I have tasted, and I may say revelled, in some new and glorious fruits, the mango, the date plum, the smooth-leaved pine, and passion fruits, stand foremost; the pears are good, but old England stands first there. No rain for twelve months round Inglewood— just fancy this. The number of gorgeous parrots in the bush is peculiar and beautiful to a stranger's eye. B—— has a capital bath-room, and every one takes one or two showers a day. It is a pretty sight to see all the children in this big bath at once, splashing, laughing, thoroughly enjoying themselves. My costume consists of riding breeches, sox, and shirt, *nothing else*, except boots, and a soft felt hat. 112° in the shade.

OPOSSUM SHOOTING—GLENELG.

4th April.—You always select a moonlight night for this sport, because these sharp little marsupials only come out after dark, and generally choose the highest branch of the tallest gum tree—this silly trick of theirs makes opossum shooting neck-aching work, and like marriage, not to be undertaken lightly. H——, B——, and I started soon after dinner (about eight o'clock), and in less than ten minutes we were in the horse paddock. Now, a bush horse paddock is generally a *small* enclosure of some 1,000 acres, close to the homestead, and covered with gum trees some 30 or 40 yards apart; a great many of these trees are ring-barked, *i.e.*, the bark is cut away in a circle about 3 feet from the ground, and in time the trees die, and stand white, staring and leafless until a sudden gust of wind sends them over—there they lie in hundreds (this killing of the trees gives the grass a chance), until decay makes them into dust. I very soon found that decay had not done its duty properly, for with my head up and eyes peering into the trees, I fell over a stump; I was *awfully lucky* in falling, for I bumped every bone in my body, upset my cartridges, sent my gun flying and had to grope for them among the stones and short grass. In this attempt I had *not* the good luck to put my hand on a sleeping snake, but an unfortunate man like myself can't expect everything, anyhow, I always carried all my cartridges in my pocket after this, and loaded *only* when I saw "pussy." H—— S——, soon called out "here you are;" so away I rushed over the dry, short slippery grass, and in my anxiety for a shot, fell into a small dry creek, barking my shins; this led to profanity. I was soon close to Harry, and could easily see my little hairy friend standing out against the moonlight. B—— said, "keep him in a line with the moon and fire." I think I did fire at the moon, for the little beggar made a horrid row, and soon hid himself in the leaves above my head. My next shot was more to the purpose, for down he came with a thud, missing my nose by about an inch. My good luck never deserted me, for I next ran against a branch of a tree, scratching my face, and bunging up an odd eye or so—and finally caught my feet in some old wire fencing, tore my inexpressibles, drove my great toe nearly through my boot! here I again said something. Anyway I killed eleven 'possums out of thirteen shots. Next day I visited my looking-glass, and as I looked, I really thought a good showman might have made something out of me, as the "Brisbane chicken after the battle." My eyes were quiet and retiring, the nose seemed out of the perpendicular, my lips had more flesh than usual—I could tell that without any glass, and a beautiful scratch made the mouth look about four inches long, my shins were very handsome, all blue and red; I can safely say, 'possum shooting, like coaching, is not monotonous. My neck seemed to belong to some one else, for it did not fit in the least. The reading of this may amuse you, but the reality hardly had that effect upon me.

A KANGAROO DRIVE.

E—— B——, being anxious to show me Australian sport, organised a drive, and I can give you my word kangaroo shooting is exciting, especially to the novice. On the morning of the day fixed, a motley group mustered in the garden paddock. Some twenty white and black men all mounted on active horses, gun on thigh, dressed in white trousers, striped shirts, broad-brimmed straw hats, their horses well bred, and capital climbers—this band to act as beaters. M——, Miss B——, Mrs. S——, H——, and I on horseback; E—— B——, driving a buggy and pair with Mrs. B——, nurse, baby, and B——; Tommy with a spring-cart containing the rest of the children, and a huge clothes' basket full of "tucker," Australian name for grub, hence "Tommy Tucker." After five miles drive through the bush the cavalcade drew up beside the bank of a creek overshadowed by gum trees, here we left the ladies and children to arrange the picnic. We men rode right away two miles or so farther into the bush. The plan of action is very simple; the kangaroos *are forced* on a line of gunners, each behind a large tree, every man stationed about 100 yards apart; each shot having tethered his horse some 150 yards behind him, quietly (and in my case somewhat nervously) awaited the game. Twenty beaters on horseback form a HUGE semicircle embracing thousands of acres, and gradually force the animals on the line of fire, and by degrees narrow the limit. My first shot was at a big wallaroo, standing some 7 or 8 feet in height.

When I fired he was bounding with enormous strides, or rather hops, towards me; he fell dead after one big jump, and I was not sorry, for these old men can rip a dog or horse clean up with one blow of their powerful hind leg, and at all times are nasty customers at close quarters. It was a curious sight to see these long-legged animals hopping along with gigantic bounds, suddenly stopping when they fancied danger. They are not so easy to hit as may be imagined, for the trees are numerous, and, according to the rules of this sport, you may only fire *right* in front and *right* behind: I can tell you the flyers hop along at a tremendous pace. In about half-an-hour the cracking of whips, yells, shouts, and the thump, thump of the game made me feel excited. Everything was going well for my position when E——'s horse broke loose; of course he was bound to follow him—this spoilt his and my sport, for mammies, veterans, wallaroos, and wallabies rushed down the open space caused by his absence and out of my range; nevertheless we did fairly well, and many a scalp hung from our horses' head-gear on our return to M——'s camp. I should tell you that the kangaroo is so numerous the Government give 8d. a head for the scalp, so you may be sure all shoot as well as possible. I think the "mammies" are the mothers, and "joeys" the little beggars in the pouch. Being all hot and dusty we mounted and returned to lunch. How much "Billy tea" I drank will remain a mystery. It was a pretty sight this bush picnic, free and easy, the beaters about 100 yards off, with horses tethered close to their hands, guns against trees, all doing justice to M——'s providing, we ourselves wiring into lobster salad, salmon and cucumber, &c., looking brown and dusty under a cloudless sky. The same kind of drive was repeated in another spot, and this time my chief show was a grizzled veteran. The whole day was novel and exciting; the gallop home through the endless bush most enjoyable. You cannot get a finer bush driver than E—— B——, his eye and knowledge are marvellous. The track winds in and out through standing trees, dead stumps, stones, rocks, and fallen trees. He goes at a very fast pace; at first you expect to be dashed against something, but his practised skill clears all bothers, and you feel half intoxicated with the glorious air and rapid pace. The mornings and evenings are crisp and cool; the days cloudless and sunny. Mid-day heat 103° in the shade.

Tipping, &c.

I have now seen the manners and customs of most countries, but in no place does this nasty habit of tipping take such a prominent place as it does in England. HERE, if you think the boots has done you an *extra* good turn, you give him 2s. 6d. or so after a week's stay; but here, thank goodness, you miss that horrid sensation of being watched away. I am sure that tipping is pernicious in the extreme. No matter where a man goes in England, he must start and finish with fees. You fee a railway porter to put your luggage in a cab; you fee the guard for a comfortable seat; you overpay the cabman. Remain a day or so at the hotel, call for the bill, and that is the signal for attack. There is the chambermaid just outside your door with a broom laid hold of for the occasion, the boy whom you never thought of asks if he may not carry down the small hand-bag for you, the boots rushes the baggage on the roof, smug waiters you never saw before stand round the hall. In my daily bill I see 1s. 6d. for service, and yet these men crowd about and make you feel uncomfortable unless you give them something. The system is bad, and the coin spent goes indirectly into the pockets of the landlords. This nuisance is not confined to hotels; go to a man's place for a dance, and there stands the girl (more frequently a hired waiter has pushed her out) ready for a tip. This horrid nuisance permeates every walk of life. Go over a charitable institution, and you fee the party showing you over. Dine at friend's house, and you fancy a fee should be given to the maid or man. If you have been in the habit of going to the same house often, and always finding the same servant there, then I don't so much mind a good 'Xmas box. No one can estimate how this system lowers the tone of hospitality. You fee the scavenger, the coalman, and so on. If a man calls with a parcel he expects a glass of ale; the postman and all expect tips—in fact, this despicable business extends more or less through every branch of life. This nuisance cannot be properly gauged, for none like to look small, consequently the employer underpays his servants and the travelling public go about in discomfort. Of course I shall *fee* until, as the Vicar of Bray says, the "times do alter;" but really the system is horrid. There is another good thing out here: you don't hear so much of that mawkish "lovey dear," "wifey dear;" endearing names in the Colonial family circle are not repulsive and generally better chosen.

CHURCHES IN THE COLONIES.

The English Church in the Colonies is mostly supported by voluntary contributions, and have little or no fund except that doled out from the Establishment at home. The contrast to the Church management here and that in England is very marked—the manner of its men so different. Here you do not see the mass of want and pauperism that exists at home side by side of wealth beyond the dream of avarice. Probably no country in the world possesses such means as England possesses for the relief of poverty and the teaching of ignorance, for the lordly generosity of past generations placed in the hands of a priestly class vast sums to be used for the physical as well as the spiritual benefit of the poor. Unfortunately but a fraction of the Churches' endowed means are devoted to the objects to which they were originally intended. The vast wealth of the Established Church, which should mainly be expended on the relief of physical distress, is practically employed in maintaining a class whose mission is to preach a "false peace to the well-to-do," and a "base content to the ill-to-do." But this priesthood are not content to deal fairly with the vast wealth entrusted to them, and originally intended for the temporal wants of the poor, for instructing those unable to pay for the commoner forms of education, and publishing to the world a true spiritual life. The Church of England as a body goes out of its way, seducing the rich to give, give, give for the multiplying of churches and endowments over the land—the bulk of all monies collected is for this purpose; not to give the bread of material benefit, not to educate the masses, for the State has taken that in hand, but to build some fancy edifice that once a week (or perhaps oftener) shall be open for a few hours for those who have suitable clothes to wear, new bonnets to show, and at least a threepenny-bit to put into the inevitable plate. In London, Bristol, and all great cities, hospital accommodation for the poor is daily proving less and less equal to the demands upon it, and yet only once a year do we hear anything for the real needs of poor suffering humanity. No! Church Extension is the selfish cry, and what does it mean but the further enrichment of a caste, more patronage for Bishops, more livings only half-endowed, and duly supplemented by the bag of bags. During the last few years, when the English farmer was suffering and landlords were remitting 10, 20, and even as much as 50 per cent. from their rents, the Clergy of the Church of England in no case allowed the fraction of a tithe to lapse. Even now it is only the fashionable Churches that really fill, the poor will not go to church, and it is always a question with new comers to a district to select the church where the best people go, and this is Religion. How can the cold propriety of the Church of England reach the masses? When we do see here and there a little moral light filtering through the terrible mass of dense darkness that envelopes huge centres, we can only think with amazement what the riches of this powerful body could really do if honestly applied. Their cry is, "Come to church;" and what does the comer find in many of these so-called Christian Churches?—why, grotesque antics that sensible people recoil from, or in many cases a formal service frequently mumbled over, thereby making the Church's splendid ritual unimpressive and worse than useless. Here the clergyman appears to be more sturdy, more manly; but even here this huge patchwork machine is gradually shaping itself to the same end, and forming itself on the same old lines. What is it all but a huge guild, so solid and powerful, that the good it does do is bound to be something, but if the funds were only fairly handled the result on the low, the dirty, the ignorant, would be incalculable. Let the Church's cry to the poor be self-reliance, self-respect, cleanly homes, and the highest self-interest, and above all, moderation—not only come to church.

There is one thing sure, however much the Bishops and clergy differ on matters of detail, or minor points of ritual—they certainly manifest a general unanimity in securing to themselves all that the law allows, and as much more as may be eloquently drawn from the public pocket.

If the Clergy had the real welfare of the masses at heart, their cry would be give, not for the multiplication of Churches over the land, but, give freely that we may build Theatres, Music Halls, Billiard Rooms, Recreation and Dancing Grounds, &c., where the poor may find occupation, amusement, and instruction. Could such be obtained and placed under manly, enlightened, and far-seeing authority, the public-house would soon become deserted, the self-satisfied patch of blue ribbon would vanish from the land, moderation would take the place of fanaticism, and drunkenness would gradually become less and less. It is this want of amusement that brutalises the English poor; amuse them, take them away from their terrible surroundings, let them have water, warmth, and wash-houses, cheap as possible, and the time may some day come when the poor will go of their own accord to Church.

The fancies of this generation will be the facts of the next.

LETTER XI.

On Board the Pacific Mail S.S. *Australia*. (Captain Ghest).

24th April.—I forget if I mentioned my visit to Jacob Kercher, the wine-grower. The old man has a small vineyard of about 90 acres under full cultivation, and some 100 or so just planted, or ready for planting. He was originally with a German grower in Europe, also his wife. Now they have a nice homestead, freehold land, cool cellars, all to themselves. Wine-growing in Australia is really of considerable importance, and men like old Jacob, with his quiet manner, general knowledge, and Colonial experience, are preparing wine not only for Australia but Europe. Some of the Colonial wines are unquestionably too powerful and doctored, also the grapes are plucked too ripe, but a careful man like our friend produces a rich wine far superior to the lower class of Burgundy, and quite pure (at least so far as this vineyard goes). The soil and climate are eminently propitious for wine-growing. Kercher's vats are beautifully clean, and I thoroughly enjoyed my smoke, chat, and homely meal with the old gentleman. As I sit in the saloon of the *Australia* I cannot help recalling incidents and impressions connected with the Colonies now left far behind. Our time, on the whole, has been spent enjoyably, and swiftly, too swiftly flown. Both have gained a large experience, and the early gloom cast over the trip is gradually wearing off. My stay in Queensland, and especially in Glenelg, impressed me more perhaps than any other portion of the tour. I shall never forget one ride with Maggie through the bush, with its blue-green foliage. We were returning from mustering some 10,000 sheep. As we rode homeward there appeared a glorious sunset on the Woolshed Hill. For a moment each sharp crag took the colour of gold, then became crimson, and finally purple. As our horses walked side by side I grasped for the first time the reality of intense solitude—so vividly marked in this Australian bush. Bare of humanity, nothing to break the stillness but the chirp of some insect, the occasional whirr of a flock of parrots, or the far away flop, flop of the heavy kangaroo. This peculiar silence and the heat became nearly oppressive. As the sun went down the crisp evening air pulled us together, creating a desire for action, so we started into a gallop, Maggie's skirts brushing the gum trees as we rode neck and neck over stony slopes encumbered with logs and brushwood, through gullies fringed with green, past water holes covered with lilies; on and on, with now and then a spice of danger to the "new chum," pulling up at last close to the boundary gate, horses panting, the riders flushed with the grand exercise. No wonder Maggie looks well. Our Colonial cousins are certainly a "long-suffering, law-abiding," good-natured people in the matter of railway travelling. The pace is slow, the carriages dirty, the jolting terrible, the porters indifferent, and the number of stoppages awful. All railways are Government property, and at holiday time the crush is fearful. I shall never fail to remember twelve solid hours spent in a dusty carriage on the festive day preceding Good Friday. The natural products of Brisbane—hospitality and mosquitoes. The glorious sunny days spent in Sydney harbour, with their picnics, fishing, and seining; the Rainswick racecourse gay with colour and splendid horses—everything so carefully thought out and easily managed, are now but memories. Of course there are a *great* many things connected with the Colonies one cannot like. The food is abundant, but, on the whole, badly cooked, and indifferently put on; the attendance *bad*. Hotel accommodation anything but good—the bedrooms are small, and by no means as clean as we find them at home—the servants and young people behind the counter are simply careless, sometimes very nearly impertinent; this is more marked in the small country stores. There is a great deal of unnecessary "blowing" or bragging of "what we have done," "how rich we are," but to an extent that may be excused, for really the wonder is how much *has been really accomplished* in so few years. I am sorry to record that drinking is *far more* marked out here than at home, and the system of " shouting" is simply nasty to a degree. Shouting means an excuse to get a drink without looking as though you were drinking for drinking's sake, by asking another to join you and expecting the same compliment later on.

The *Australia* of the Pacific Mail Co. is a long narrow ship of some 3,000 tons, fairly comfortable, but all day long she has been rolling terribly, and many a good man has cast his bread upon the waters, neither caring nor hoping for a return, and one poor lady next cabin to ours has suffered in an alarming manner. My left hand companion at table (for of course L—— always sits on óne side) is a very pretty girl, and the greatest flirt I have ever come across. I apologised for not being younger, and offered to give place to her selection, but she deigned to tell me I did very well indeed as a dinner companion. Her father, Captain M——, is a decent old sort, and altogether I must not grumble at my place. The rolling during the night was bad—hardly any real sleep for the best of us. The water got into somebody's cabin, the male belonging to the same continued saying all manner of polite things in an audible voice, and howling for the steward. Boxes and bags were sliding about; groaning and noises all over the ship; all the empty water-cans in the passage met in one big bang outside our door, then tumbled over each other, and finally skuttled off to pay another call. Few were at breakfast, and all looked jolly cross. I think we have the champion snorer of New Zealand close to us—he has already forced his cabin companion to sleep on deck—he makes night hideous by terrific noises. Yesterday, being April the 30th, was Wednesday, and as Thursday is May the 1st, we put in an extra Thursday as we were crossing 180°, for of course you know we gain a day in going round the world. The *Australia* averages 300 knots, and is fairly comfortable; but our cabin companion is a stick and lout. We danced in the saloon last night with the thermometer 90°. I don't remember ever having such hard work. I helped as M.C.; and had it not been for Captain Ghest, our skipper, a bright handsome man, I should have been knocked up. Did I tell you L—— sent all my Sydney letters to B——'s in Queensland. They could not be returned in time to catch me, so H—— S—— will bring them home. This was a nuisance.

4th May.—A heavy but lazy roll; a warm moist heat, about 90° in cabin—everybody limp. Passed the windward island of the Navigator group—stopped close alongside—we were boarded by dusky natives selling bananas. The islands are wooded to the water's edge and intensely emerald in green.

Often as I did the "block" in Sydney, I stopped at the Post Office, noting the throng under its fine stone portico. The anxious faces grouped round the opening for "letters to be called for" afforded plenty of scope for the imagination. The "new chum" with his batch of welcome letters striding away with pleased smile; the unsuccessful man, awaiting perhaps a father or a brother's help, wearied by constant " none this mail;" the settler's wife anxious for news from mother or loved sister at home. I fancied I could in some way guess each one's business—a smile, a frown, a muttered curse, a half blush, gave a good criterion of the inner thoughts, and I think I really felt how very dear dear this endless chain of human hopes and fears must be, extending from the mother country "home" to her daughter "Colony." "It is difficult to over-estimate the emotions set at work by the European mail, and half an hour spent under the portico of a large Colonial Post Office should tell how close and real are the ties between England and her pioneer children."

5th May.—Very muggy, close, and hot. I can tell you it was hard work managing the Wax-works last night.

The Chamber of Beauty consisted of Marie Antoinette, a Nun, Peasant, Queen Elizabeth (very good), Ophelia, a lady with golden hair below her knees, Grace Darling, &c. The Chamber of Horrors, Ned Kelly, Richard Third, Spotted Baby from Peru, The Ghost in Hamlet, &c., &c. We opened up with the "Star-spangled Banner" and "Rule Britannia" in Figure. Four tableaux. "Where are you going to, my pretty maid?" "Smothering of the Princes in the Tower," &c. But what took the audience most, "The Babes in the Wood." We have five *very* pretty children on board. We knocked up some scenery, and posed them as two sleeping children, and three angels watching over, &c. Then down went the curtain, and two HUGE men, both six feet, were exhibited, dressed as babies, in drawers and night-gowns, eating two huge buns. These were the "*Real* Babies," and created lots of fun. The last tableaux. "Blue

Beard and his Wives." The ladies of the company stood behind a sheet brought close to the neck. Blue Beard stood in front, with his last wife kneeling and holding the bloody keys—the whole lighted with blue fire. Although I had something to do with management, I must say the thing went with a capital swing—Mrs. Jarley, the Show*man*, being very good. Lord and Lady Normanby were very pleased, and paid the management no end of compliments. We have generally arranged for concerts or dances to come off nearly every night, and the voyage has been unusually pleasant. We steamed into Honolulu on Sunday, the 11th May, about 2.30 P.M., and the appearance of the island, with its lava-stained hills reflecting the tropical sun, giving back tints of orange, pink, yellow, red, brown, and drab, was more than striking, the lower slopes of brilliant green, edged with surf, and bounded by the deepest of blue seas, forming in all a fascinating picture. Our run ashore was short, but we managed to see a little. Some of the natives are very fine men, and the women handsome.

The gambling on board is very considerable, but not more than usual. The old steamer is daily getting lighter, and every now and then she rolls heavily. This morning I was standing in the bath finishing the towel part, when a wave rushed through the port, and that, with the lurch, sent me clean out of the bath, and I fell in a heap in the corner, striking my head. I soon pulled myself together, but I still feel the shock. To-day for the first time since starting I may say my appetite has been hardly trustworthy, and I feel dull and heavy. We had "Cox and Box" for the evening's entertainment. It was a grand success. The prologue (a humorous rhyme on the events of the voyage) created a bit of amusement; the reader (a rough diamond) I pushed into my dress clothes:—

R.M.S. *AUSTRALIA*—THEATRE ROYAL.

Lessee and Manager, . .	*Mr. H. B. Tucker.*
Stage Manager, . . .	*Mr. B. C. Harriman.*
Assistant Stage Manager, .	*Mr. C. M. Crompton-Roberts.*

PROGRAMME.
May 16, 1884.
COX AND BOX.
Triumviretta in One Act, by F. C. Burnand and Sir Arthur Sullivan.

James John Cox (*a Journeyman Hatter*), . . Mr. MacLachlan.
John James Box (*a Journeyman Printer*), . . Mr. T. P. Royle.
Serjeant Bouncer, { (Late of the Dampshire Yeomanry, and with Military reminiscences), } Rev. W. Jervois.

Accompanist, Miss C. Reid.

To be preceded at 8.30 by
A PROLOGUE,
Written by Mr. J. S. M'Arthur.
To be delivered by Mr. J. Gough.

Excuse, dear friends, our venturous act,
And view our fiction as a fact.
Believe we give our "*little all,*"
And don't be vexed because it's small.
The previous sights that you have seen
Will in your memories still be green ;
Nor from Japan to fair Neuralia,

Has been such fun as on the *Australia*.
You'll long remember Mrs. Jarley,
And smile as you recall her parley,
Recalling, 'mid your cares and duty,
Some memories of the Room of Beauty;
And how, within the Ruffian's Ring,
A *Senator* became a *King!*
Marie Antoinette, Ned Kelly,
And Bluebeard in the general mêlée.
If in this Prologue haps a *bull*,
Remember we've been *toss'd* to the full.
Our captain, as our *host* and *Ghest*,
Has, to amuse us, done his best,
And shown that Sports and Jollity
May oft be found upon the sea.
Here ladies raced each with potato,
And "*Donald Dinnie*" put the weight-oh!
The cock-fights put some on their back,
And many others "got the *Sack*."
Whilst Tugs-of-War 'twixt weight and muscle
Resulted each in sturdy tussle.
The Ladies would not take the bother
To *spoon* about with one another,
Except a few who in the race
Displayed their usual skill and grace.
Their little *chickens* though were fain
To run for cake though not for *grain*.
And then the Captain got "A Nipper,"
For every *girl* became a *Skipper;*
And their hopes leant "upon a Reed"
Who did not fail in time of need.
The victor's prizes—made of *tin*—
Were giv'n away the saloon within,
Amidst the plaudits of the fair,
Who in full force were gathered there.

We'd *swells* and *boobies* hovering near,
But none on board I will aver!
The sweepstakes were a great success.
If you'd believe the earnestness
Of those who lucky were and won,
You'd think they were the greatest fun.
Although we'd *squalls above*, you know
The *squalls* were sweeter far *below*;
(We mean this as a compliment
To those who have so kindly lent
Their voices, and their aid have given,
To render the saloon a heaven).
A dance was held, and all must feel
The most appropriate was "a Reel;"
But, ah! too soon the hours fled,
Till, with regret, "good-night" was said.
But good things cannot last for ever,
And soon the best of friends must sever;
And soon we hope to have a frisk-oh,
Without the slightest chance of risk-oh!
Upon the fair shores of Ameriky—
(At the bad joke don't get hysteriky!)
We've spoken of the Captain, and
We now must praise his gallant band
Of Officers, who kindly tried
To spread amusement far and wide
With jest and *quilp*—(we do not mean
That any one like *Quilp* was seen!)
Some members, too, formed a Committee,
In which were skilful hands and witty.
And often they have given us cause
To honour them with our applause.
They hope the last fun they present
Will send you all away content.
The little farce is *Cox and Box*,

Composed of jokes, and songs, and knocks.
Two angry gentlemen discover
Each has been fighting with his brother.
With various incidents the play
Amuses both the grave and gay.
The actors have worked hard for days,
And well deserve the highest praise.
And now my prologue's nearly done;
But first I must allude to one
By whose consent the play is played,
By whose consent the scenes are made—
We all give thanks to Captain Ghest,
And hope his life may long be blest;
And, if again we put to sea,
May we find captains good as he!
To captain, officers, and crew
Our very hearty thanks are due;
We give you all this parting greeting—
And here's to our next merry meeting!!

The old ship rolls very heavily, but now none thinks of it. We are expecting to reach San Francisco in about twenty-four hours, so all are busy packing, &c. The voyage of the *Australia* has been very pleasant and full of "go."

LETTER XII.

SAN FRANCISCO, CALIFORNIA, &C.

WE had a jollification the last night on board the *Australia* —suppers and "sparkling," finishing up with " Auld Lang

Syne," &c. Early next morning we passed the customs, sent luggage to Palace Hotel by Express, and took tram there ourselves; this is the cheapest and best way. It is well to start *from* the ship with a little American money for trams, which may be obtained of the barman. San Francisco is a wonderful place—a city of gigantic contrasts —the huge Palace Hotel and the horrid den of the " Heathen Chinee," 32 feet below the level of the ground; magnificent shops alongside a ten cent. show; rubbishy jewellery next door to a store containing some of the most marvellous and costly gold and silver work I have ever seen. The Chinese quarter (40,000) is deeply curious, but hardly amusing. I shall never forget going into the opium dens, filthy boxes under the level of the city—here the Celestials lie and smoke themselves into deadly sleep; the Chinese Theatre with its crowd of interested watchers—the men separate from the women—the play goes on in *different* acts for six weeks or more. We went behind the scenes, and the peculiar get-up, the horrid din of the cymbals, the beating of the tom-tom, made a hasty retreat desirable. We took wire-tram to Cliff House, and were fortunate enough to see the celebrated " sea lions" in great quantities—in fact, the rocks were covered—some huge old fellows with thick manes must have been 15 or 20 feet in length. Mr. M'Kay, the Pacific and Burlington agent, 32 Montgomery Street, B. Q. & C. (Champion Baggage Smashers), will put all travellers up to sight-seeing, and is a most useful man. The Golden Gates (the narrow entrance to the Harbour) is a very beautiful picture.

Having spent two or three days in 'Frisco, we started at 3.30 p.m. for the Yo-semite Valley. A ponderous steam Ferry took us to the Oakland Station, and soon we were settled in a fairly comfortable sleeping-car, with Captain Ghest and one or two other men from the *Australia*. We only carried hand-bags and a rug—the latter useless. (A light M'Intosh may be useful for getting near the Falls). The baggage we sent on to Ogden. We turned into bed shortly after ten, and slept fairly well until 3.30 a.m., when we were "hurried up" at Madera for breakfast. Madera is 182 miles from 'Frisco.

Soon after four we were all fixed in a comfortable coach with strong wheels, solid leather springs, drawn by six horses. At first the track lay over a low sandy plain, undulating in places, sparsely timbered with Californian oak. Every now and again we passed a Ranche (Farmhouse), or an occasional team of mules, with bells jingling in the morning air. For miles and miles we drove parallel to a wooden aqueduct or "flume," used for floating timber down from the Sierra Nevada. Upon inquiry I found it extended for over fifty miles. California is very rich in wheat, and this season especially so; the export will be enormous, for the rains have fallen over nearly all parts. The sward is covered with flowers of all kinds, and once or twice we saw a creeping plant with a flower so peculiar that a man like Oscar Wilde would go mad over its beauty. Picture a huge corrugated convolvulus, pale lavender in colour, deepening in the centre to a dark purple, 9 inches across—that perhaps may give you some idea. Right and left large bushes of buckeye (a small tree with white flower, something like the wild chestnut—its perfume being like a mild stephanotis). Less than a fortnight ago this very coach, with the same driver, was "bailed up" and robbed by a gang of men in broad daylight—every mortal thing carried off—dollars, studs, rings, and watches. Two men stood on rising ground, close to the coach, with double-barrelled guns covering the party, whilst two others with revolvers cleared the lot. These "cow boys" are still at large. We passed bunches of poisoned oak—a plant so deadly that during its seed-time many by simply passing and inhaling the poison have been so affected as to swell in every joint. We lunched at Coarse Gold Gulch, a spot where a big rush was once made, and no less than 1,000,000 dollars worth of gold was taken out from a very small space of earth. On and on through beautiful glades of black oak, across shallow fords, jolting and jumping, the road itself only a shade better than those in New Zealand—past fir trees, with cones from 9 to 12 inches in length, towering 150 to 250 feet into the sky. After another hour's travelling, the incline became steeper, the track worse, the pace a walk, and the ascent of the Sierra Nevada commenced.

The road wound in and out through rich valleys of pale green undergrowth, dotted with groups of graceful firs. The sun was bright, the air keen, but the roads, owing to recent rains, were heavy and sticky. Higher and higher, the track leading through lofty pine forests, every now and then we could see the summit, partially covered in cloud. It was tedious work, but the views were most beautiful; many of the pine trees stood out brown and bare, the branches enveloped with *yellow green* moss, giving a vivid contrast to the dull colour of the darker firs. Still upwards, and just about dusk we felt the crisp air from the snow-covered mountains. The road soon became nearly impassable, the coach was either stationary, or groaning and creaking dismally, the poor horses steaming and pulling, the driver swearing and cracking his whip. As evening drew on the forest became quite dense, the road worse, and all had visions of being landed for the night without food, and, what was worse, without any whisky between us. At a quarter to eight we made our last change of horses, lighted our lamps, warmed our hands, and finally drove in the dark to Clark's Hotel, where we arrived at 9.30 a.m., having been over seventeen hours in the coach doing seventy-five miles, with relays of no less than thirty-six horses. A warm over a cheerful wood-fire, a supper, and a welcome glass of toddy, pulled us together; soon sleep, gentle sleep, came o'er us.

Up at five o'clock, a keen frosty air rushed into the room as I opened my window, the water being cold enough to make my fingers tingle. Our coach for the Yo-semite was not quite so easy as that of the preceding day, nevertheless, at the order "all aboard," we managed to tumble together. For the first hour the track lay alongside a rapid river, with trunks of trees dashed here and there, or stranded beside the road—"as the tree falls, so it lies," for no man troubles to remove fallen timber here. Gradually we made our way upwards, the horses dragging the heavy coach through a regular slough of thick clinging mud, frequently up to the axle-tree. In fine weather the track may be good enough, but just now it was simply awful; in passing one horrid place we could see, wedged into the rocks below, the dead body of a coach-horse, the bay-coloured skin quite distinct in the sunlight. The accident only happened a short time back, but fortunately none of the passengers were injured. On, slowly on, at something under three miles an hour, through groves of lofty pines, with here and there a group of cinnamon-coloured firs, their long branches feathered with bright yellow-green lichen, affording a curious and beautiful contrast to the dark forest. The bright-eyed gray squirrels gave life to the scene. Fortunately we carried spades, for about mid-day the first coach stuck up—nothing could move it, so it was literally dug out. I ought to mention the trifling fact that a trace and splinter-bar were also smashed. We should have been totally without food had not one of the passengers luckily brought a hamper with him from 'Frisco, and, with a traveller's liberality, divided it. The drive was most tiresome and tedious. We arrived at Bernard's Hotel at 5.30, having taken the whole day (of twelve hours) doing twenty-four miles.

YO-SEMITE VALLEY.

The only alloy to me when I see such grand sights as the Yo-semite Valley is the fact that I cannot have all those I care for round me to enjoy the wonders of nature, but as that may not be, I will do my best to describe this matchless place, and only wish I had not used such powerful language in other places, for now I really require many adjectives and words I used long ago. I want you first to imagine an irregular valley some fifteen miles in length, and about a mile or less in width; the base a *perfectly flat-lying* plateau between two enormous masses of rock some 4,000 feet high, the bright green turf dotted with every variety of tree. The waterfalls in this valley are higher and larger than any I have ever seen or imagined. Just now we are seeing them at their very best, for the melting snow and late rains have filled the rivers. The Yo-semite Fall itself thunders down 2,634 feet into the valley below, causing a rumble like the roar of distant artillery, forming, with the Nevada Falls, the rapid Merced River.

Bernard's Hotel is comfortable, and our party have possession of the "Cottage." Last night the rats had possession of our boots, and every bit of kid was removed. The general sitting-room, with its cheerful log-fire, is built round a huge tree some seven feet in diameter, 175 in height; it is a white cedar, and very rare.

MIRROR LAKE AND NEVADA FALLS.

On the day following we started at 7.30 for Mirror Lake—a party of eleven. The morning was simply perfection. Our drive to the end of the valley, where the Mirror Lake rests, took us through groves of maple, sugar pine, firs, and pines. Every now and then we noticed the dogwood tree, or rather bush, laden with a pale-green flower, something like a fully-opened Christmas rose; past little islands covered with huge firs, shining like burnished copper in the morning sun, and surrounded by a seething mass of yellow foam. We alighted and walked round the border of this perfectly placid lake; no wind to ruffle its surface. The truly marvellous effect of the reflection cannot be put in words; each leaf and rock, each mountain and waterfall mirrored in its depths. The Half Dome, with its bare scalp, stood 3,568 feet above us, and again beneath us, in the water, Cloud's Rest, with its snow-capped top miles away, yet just at our feet. A mare and foal grazing on the bank were truly photographed in colour and form, adding something of warmth to the picture. Killarney, Lucerne, Loch Katrine, are not forgotten, but their waters never had the opportunity of reflecting such gigantic masses or such lofty trees as this tiny lake at the far end of the Yo-semite Valley. A short drive back brought us to the point where horses met us for the ascent of the Nevada Falls. Another party of some dozen or more joined us. Such a motley turn out I never witnessed. All the animals had the huge Mexican saddle, nearly all more or less worn out, with wooden stirrups and high pommels. Everybody seemed to be on the wrong beast—fat men on lean horses, tall men on ponies, short chubby men on huge bony animals, ladies on mules, every variety of hat from the smoke-stack to the pork-pie, every kind of face from the hatchet-faced Yankee to the bonnie maiden of "bashful eighteen." After a long, slow, single-file clamber and many a rest, we reached a wooden house at the foot of the Nevada Falls; hardly off our horses when away they rushed to the stables without a word from any one. Some of the party made for the top, but the heat was rather against that, so two or three of us, myself among the number, scrambled in, over, and between huge granite boulders to the base of this grand fall. Although we got very wet, *nobody cared;* the fierce rush of the water, the bright morning sun, the crisp air, the rich smell of pine trees, made all feel careless of trouble or slight annoyances. The enormous mass of granite over which this rush of water dashes is crescent-shaped, and continues far beyond the actual space taken up by the fall, and has many tiny cascades falling from the same height as the main body; these are blown into clouds of spray long before they reach the bottom, forming rainbows of every size. From the position we took the long branches of the sombre pines formed a green fringe to this cream-coloured fall. The main fall is eighty feet wide at the top, eight feet thick, and drops in one rush 700 feet into a rocky basin beneath. You cannot get very near, for the dense spray forms a misty vapour, being carried by the wind for a long distance. I lugged and tugged a merry little Yankee girl through holes and over slippery rocks, and both were pretty well tired, and when we arrived at the chalet we were ready and willing for luncheon. After lunch I strolled to the head of the Vernal Falls. Here nature has formed a complete buttress of granite CLOSE to where the rush of water takes its final leap of 350 feet. You can look over into the valley beneath and trace the winding river 1,200 feet below, the walls of rock forming a complete amphitheatre. I christened my brute "Slippery Jack," for every now and then he gave a nasty slip, and not being anxious to arrive before the others, I got off and walked, feeling pleased upon reaching the bottom. Here a dozen or more started off into a gallop. Oh, dear! such a gallop. Helter-skelter along the dirty road, some holding on by the pommel, others holding on to hats. One mule got rid of his rider, and kicked away in the most happy manner, finally kicking himself clear of his saddle. The queer figures some of the riders cut is quite beyond me, and fit only for Mark Twain. Ladies can do this trip very well indeed, for the path is fairly good—only dangerous in one or two places. Cost of carriage and horse for each person for the whole day, 4 dollars 80 cents, or about £1.

I am not quite certain whether I gave you to understand that the bottom of this marvellous valley is 4,060 feet above the level of the sea, consequently the average height of these nearly, and in some cases, quite, perpendicular cliffs, is over 7,000 feet. On Monday we selected horses in order to make Glacier Point, but luckily a misty rain came on in time to stay our starting and avoid the great danger of being out on the "trail" in a fog. We hired a carriage, and drove from our "cottage" to the Cascade end of the Valley. The first object of interest we passed was the Yo-semite Falls (the name is Indian, and means Great Grizzly Bear). This fall is supposed to be the highest fall of any magnitude in the world—2,634 feet in all. The first drop of 1,600 feet dashes into a cavern 30 yards deep by 20 wide, and immediately on with a roar like thunder for another mad drop of 534 feet, and finally rushes over 500 feet into the valley below. Just now the volume of water is very heavy, for the powerful sun is rapidly melting the miles and miles of snow-fields, and that, coupled with the late rain, creates so big a body of water that more than three-fourths of a mile away the window panes rattle again. We drove quietly onward through an emerald plain, dotted with colour, bright with baby pine trees, whose tender shoots are shielded from the sun by giant brothers towering 150 feet above. This park-like grove is level as an English lawn, and full of curious wild flowers—the most conspicuous being the *yellow* violet, the carmine snow-plant, the *scarlet* ragged-robin, the blue lupen, and long armed clematis, pushing their young life through a rich alluvial soil. I cannot tell you the names of half the fine timber one sees here—the maple, the sugar pine, the silver fir, the live oak, the red-barked manganista, the tree laurel, and dozens of others are made into most artistic cabinets by A. Sinning, a clever German, and although at first the price appears high, as a work of art they are cheap. Nearly every tree has its merry little squirrel, or perhaps the red-capped woodpecker calls attention to its industry, for many and many a tree is simply a series of perforations caused by its sharp and determined beak. Gaudy butterflies chase each other in the warm sunlight, while from every crag pours a network of silver chains, like fine Norwegian filigree work. Past the pointed Sentinel, 3,100 feet above; under the frowning cliffs called by the Indians, Pom-pom-pa-sus, or Three Brothers, 3,900 feet in height, and next, "El Capitan," "the Monarch of the Glen," stands out in bold relief, rising 3,300 feet in one huge mass of perpendicular rock. As we skirted its base, one and a quarter miles in length, we could see huge boulders covering the ground—many split in half by the terrific fall from the height above. A little farther, in a deep dark recess, Lung-oo-too-koo-ya (tall and slender), but generally known as the Widow's Tears, from the fact that the water dries up in a month or six weeks after the commencement of the thaw, falls in graceful folds some 3,300 feet. Just now it is very beautiful, but the snow will soon melt, and this fine fall will become a tiny thread. Here and there wigwams inhabited by the dirty but picturesque Digger Indian. Very soon the valley widens, and the Merced moves swiftly but smoothly along, when *quite abruptly* the huge cliffs close in, the valley becomes a chasm, the dark river one seething mass of white foam, the creamy water one turbulent rush, charging over blocks of granite, dead pine trees, hurrying smaller timber round and round in rapid eddies. For over a mile the Merced is no longer a river, but one wild cataract. Suddenly a sharp curve terminates the valley, and the Merced disappears from view, making the other end of this incomparable valley a striking contrast to the placid Mirror Lake. Towards noon the rain came steadily down, so we took refuge in a partly-finished cottage, and enjoyed the contents of a picnic basket, and, with a fragrant weed, admired the beauties of the "Cascade," a broad and prettily forked body of water that anywhere else would call for rapture. Even the drive back beneath the dripping trees meant enjoyment, for everything was so fresh—the odour of the pine trees so pleasant, the gloss on the young leaves so bright, and soon even the slightest trace of discomfort was quite forgotten, as the Bridal Veil Fall literally burst into view. This beautiful, and, one may safely say, unrivalled fall has a clear drop of 900 feet, and although the height is small compared with others in Yo-semite, its charming outline entitles it to be called the "Gem of the Valley." We were fortunate in seeing its creamy glory influenced by a breeze, the edges falling in irregular waves on the moss-covered boulders below—as the sun shone through the volume of mist, fairy rainbows added to the effect. The golden-tinted Cathedral Spires, 2,660 feet in height, stood out between the sombre pines—in the distance the snow-covered "Clouds' Rest,"

6,150, stands, a stately guardian over the placid Mirror Lake.

We had our photographs taken, but I fear all in the group will not come out well, for many were on the broad grin, and for my own part I know I must have worn three distinct expressions during the operation. I rather fancy myself the culprit. The photographs by Fiske are good, and Miss Abbie, the daughter of the landlord, gave us a lot of information in a most pleasant way. The best time to see the Yo-semite may be fixed from May the 20th to June 20th, or from September 1st to October 1st. You may think I have somewhat overdrawn my pictures, but such is far from the fact. I have seen the best of Switzerland, Norway, Apennines, Canada, New Zealand, but for massive grandeur the Yo-semite Valley bears the palm, and although the discomfort was real, the return was worth all the cost and annoyance.

With regret we said good-bye to the valley and its kindly inmates, and started at 5.30 a.m. in a keen frosty air, that, with the misty atmosphere, made ulsters useful, but when we reached Inspiration Point the sun was holding possession; and in remembering our farewell to this charming spot, the beautiful "Cascade," rich in the most vivid of opal tints, will be the final memory. The return journey was a trifle better than going, but to any one not absolutely strong the jolting and bucking was trying and back-aching. We reached Clarke's about two, where we gained the pleasant information that four men would have to go on straight, and at once to Merced, the thirteen remaining to be crammed into a through coach starting at five next morning. We made no end of a row, but all to no purpose. The proprietors are humbugs, and we told them so. At first they were plausible, then independent. They know they have you in their power. In future I would go *via Merced*, avoiding the long stage and Clarke's Hotel like poison. Four elected to go *via* Merced, where they arrived at midnight, having travelled in a coach over nineteen hours, with only one rest of half-an-hour. The remainder of the party drove in the afternoon to Mariposa Grove to see the "Big Trees," and nothing will ever efface from my memory this short but truly horrid drive. The poor horses dragged and tugged the coach over a track nothing less than one continuous bog, rutty and uneven—talking was more than difficult, and smoking simply dangerous—thank goodness it was a short stage of only seven miles. We had two coaches, consequently only a couple in each seat, therefore we were tossed, bumped, bucked, bruised, and generally annoyed; and to cap the lot, we could not *drive through* the celebrated Tree, for it was filled up with frozen snow, but, thank goodness, we saw numbers of fine trees, many nearly 300 feet in height. We spent some time under the "Grizzly Giant." This gigantic specimen of "Sequoia Gigantea," or Wellingtonia, is a species of cedar measuring 99 feet in circumference, with a diameter fairly measured at 33 feet. This aged gentleman stretches out his first arm 80 feet from the ground, and this alone measures 6 feet through. We joined hands, the arms being stretched to the fullest extent, and at 5 feet from the ground it took over fifteen men to span it. Two or three specialists have used the ordinary calculations in such cases, and they give 6,000 years as the lowest computation of its age. What a grand thing it would be for Conservatives if old Gladstone took a freak into his head to fell this tawny giant, and relieve England of his presence until the work was completed.

The return journey to Clarke's was a simple repetition of groans, and more frequently a British exclamation told how some long-suffering head had come into contact with the roof. This short stage was too bad for words, worse than any of our New Zealand experiences. The horses were well-bred, strong, and full of pluck.

On the bright frosty morning of *May 28th* the thirteen unfortunates met at the door of Clarke's about 5.30. After some considerable delay, and by no means gracious language, we jammed ourselves into the coach—the word jam is hardly strong enough to convey how crushed and close we were. The men who run these coaches are not scrupulous, and I should avoid placing myself in the hands of such dollar-scraping rascals. The pain and discomfort was next to unbearable, but "every cloud has a silver lining," and the great weight in the coach made the jolting and tossing somewhat less—a beautiful day with a warm sun made even the bruised ones to rejoice. On the far side of the Sierra Nevada the roads were dry, the pace good, but here and there the dust gave us a new experience. To add to our misery, a fat old Jew man kept bumming or humming in a thick greasy voice the most dismal of airs, and this he continued for hours. We did our best to be jolly, and many old heirlooms in the form of long-forgotten tales found their way to the surface. We reached Madera at 9.15, after fourteen hours' hard travelling. Slept the night in a railway car drawn up on a siding, and at two o'clock p.m. next day we reached Sacramento.

SACRAMENTO

is the capital of California, and semi-Mexican in appearance and customs. It is the oldest city of the territory, with a population of 42,000. Government House is a really fine building, but everything about the city has a "sleepy hollow" sort of look. Here we all enjoyed the much-needed luxury of a hot bath. The proprietor of the Station Buffet beguiled us into taking a large picnic basket for the long railway journey to Ogden. Although we regularly enjoyed the fun of having our breakfast and supper in the car, it was a nuisance and quite unnecessary —all should carry a full whisky flask.

OGDEN, SALT LAKE CITY.

The resources of science and civilisation have of recent years been wonderfully utilised in perfecting our means of travel. Health, comfort, and speed have been studied with such advantage that even the latest of generations which have passed away would be filled with astonishment could they look in upon us now. The passage from Liverpool to New York has been accomplished in less than seven days by the *Oregon*. Life is so short that anything that sensibly reduces the time spent in locomotion is a matter of great importance. But while we may congratulate ourselves on the unparalleled progress in the directions indicated, I doubt very much whether the measures for the real safety of passengers have kept pace with the development of speed and comfort. This is remarkably apparent in the Rio Grande Railway, a new line reaching from Ogden to Denver, a distance of 771 miles. The line is three-feet gauge, and fastened to the sleepers in the most rough-and-ready manner. I can only say, more dangerous-looking travelling I never beheld. Although the water-courses are subject to periodical rushes of snow-water, the bridges are of the flimsiest, and "wash-outs" are of constant, or rather frequent, occurrence. I have travelled over lines in a great many countries, but have never yet met with so shoddy and badly-managed a railway. In one or two places the scenery is fine and grand, especially in the Black Cañon and Royal Gorge, but not worth the risk of delay, *or worse*. (As I am copying this from my rough notes, I find from Mr. C—— the boiler of the engine in the train following us burst in atoms; nobody killed, but two men injured.) The officers of the line are, to say the least of it, indifferent. The caretaker of the Pullman car might generally be found sprawling at length in the most comfortable seat in the carriage. As for taking the word of a railway agent in America, the thing would be ridiculous, for they are the most plausible liars it has been my luck to meet. The only way to travel without expense or bother is to do as the Yankees do—sleep in your day shirts and trousers, leave off shaving, and let washing be a promise. This won't do for Englishmen; but, at the same time, I do advise everyone to travel with one small hand-bag, and that one bag to contain ALL required for the overland trip to New York from the Pacific. Porters are hard to procure, and moving luggage expensive. Book through all heavy luggage to *destination*. One old gentleman we met at Salt Lake City told us that in travelling over the Rio Grande Line he always carried "his gun, his pole (fishing-rod), and a good big hamper, for," said he, "we generally have real good long rests."

SALT LAKE CITY.

Metropolitan Hotel cheap, clean, and comfortable. The city itself is fairly well planned, but by no means finished. The inhabitants seem happy, but the women are devoid of good looks. The Temple is a marvellous place for sound, and will hold 10,000 people, and you can hear a pin drop on the carpet from the extreme end. This "Rocky Mountain Zion" is something like an English market town.

We left Salt Lake City at 9.30 on Sunday; had a very good view of Salt Lake itself from the cars. The water is very strong, and three buckets of it will make one bucket of salt.

The length is abouty 80 miles. Beyond the city the track lies through a fertile plain, from whence the broken crests of the Wasatch Mountains rise abruptly, just now covered a third of the way down with snow. Near the centre of Salt Lake Basin we passed the fresh water Utah Lake, and I am told it is literally swarming with fish. Near at hand deer and bear can be met with. Proceeding parallel to the River Jordan a low divide is reached, and Utah Valley is entered full of comfortable-*looking homes* and well tilled farms. We lunched at Provo, and thoroughly enjoyed a nice clean meal, the pastry being simply delicious. On and on until we arrived at Castle Gate, where huge rocks in places only *twenty feet* thick, just like some old castle tower, rise 500 feet in height, standing out in bold relief, and nearly barring the narrow defile. Next morning I awoke with a chilly feeling, and found we had been stuck up in the water for five hours. Soon after we pushed on, but only to find ourselves really barred, this time by a serious "wash-out" at a bridge. A large gap had been forced away between the buttresses and the bank; the rush of water through the opening was tremendous. Here we stuck all day with nothing to eat and only cold water to drink. We called the wretched place Starvation Flat. We only had an egg and salt; no bread for 27 hours. One sporting man shot a rabbit, and after cooking it over a wood fire, polished it off with the guard's assistance and the additional help of a lady and child. The man was a good shot with a revolver, and I saw him kill a rabbit running with four shots.

They could not mend the line fit for the engine to pass, so we waited for the down train, and walked with our small bags, &c., over a wretchedly ricketty bridge, everything from our train being transhipped, and, of course, *vice versa*. After a slow, cautious drive, we reached Cimarron, and made the most of a very poor meal. Here a wire informed the guard that the line ahead was in a dangerous state, so we slept there for the night and did not start for the Black Cañon of the Cimarron until twelve next day, now being 37 hours late. In one place I saw the remains of a freight train— three waggons lying in a confused heap in the river-bed; when this accident happened the driver and stoker were both killed. The Black Cañon was a grand and wild sight, the swollen river, a tumbled mass of dark-brown water, filling the whole of the narrow channel except the part raised up with rubble for the metals. Frequently we were covered with spray from the small falls, for our party stood on the back of the Pullman. The rocks are very rugged, and appear to be crumbling away; their height about double the Clifton Rocks. We ran for miles within a foot or so of the River Gunnison, and expected a wash-out every minute. After some anxiety we reached Sargent. Here, although very hungry, the food was left, being high and unwholesome. Soon we were pushing slowly up the Marshall Pass, the metals running 10,858 feet above the level of the sea, and cutting clean through the Rocky Mountains. This, I believe, is the highest railway in the world. In less than a quarter of an hour after commencing the ascent, we ran into an avalanche of mud and rock that had just fallen from the top. Passengers and officials all set to work removing the débris, and once again we resumed our slow, cautious, but by no means monotonous progress. Still upwards, $\frac{1}{20}$, $\frac{1}{30}$, through enormous snow-sheds, and winding about in the most wonderful manner. In advancing the last half mile it took seven miles of metal, and just three-quarters of an hour to do it in. At last, we made the summit, and here all got out for a stretch. This spot is called the Great Continental Divide — the rivers flow east to the Atlantic and west to the Pacific. A more wild, desolate spot I have never looked upon—snow-covered hills in every direction, and apparently close at hand is seen Mount Ouray, 14,043 feet; while whole forests of leafless firs, killed by accidental fires, added yet another uncanny element to this most dismal but fascinating scene.

Highest and Greatest Mountains in the World.

NAME.	COUNTRY.	Feet High.	Miles.
Mt. Everest (Himalayas)	Thibet	29,002	5¼
Sorato, the highest in America	Bolivia	21,284	4
Illimani	Bolivia	21,145	4
Chimborazo	Ecuador	21,422	4⅔
Hindoo-Koosh	Afghanistan	20,600	3¾
Demavend, highest of Elburz Mts.	Persia	20,000	3¾
Cotopaxi, highest volcano in world	Ecuador	19,496	3¾
Antisana	Ecuador	19,150	3½
St. Elias, highest in North America	Alaska	17,850	3⅓
Popocatapetl, volcano	Mexico	17,540	3⅓
Mt. Roa, highest in Oceanica	Hawaii	16,000	3
Mt. Brown, highest peak of Rocky Mts	Brit. America	15,900	3

NAME.	COUNTRY.	Feet. High.	Miles.
Mont Blanc, highest in Europe, Alps	Savoy	15,732	3
Mt. Rosa, next highest peak of Alps	Savoy	15,150	2⅞
Limit of perpetual snow at the	Equator	15,207	2⅞
Pichinca	Ecuador	15,924	3
Mt. Whitney	California	14,887	2¾
Mt. Fairweather	Alaska	14,500	2¾
Mt. Shasta	California	14,442	2¾
Mt. Ranier	Wash. Territ'y	14,444	2¾
Long's Peak, Rocky Mountains	Colorado	14,271	2⅔
Mt. Ararat	Armenia	14,320	2⅔
Pike's Peak	Colorado	14,216	2⅔
Mt. Ophir	Sumatra	13,800	2⅝
Fremont's Peak, Rocky Mountains	Wyoming	13,570	2⅝
Mt. St. Helens	Wash. Territ'y	13,400	2½
Peak of Teneriffe	Canaries	12,182	2⅛
Miltzin, highest of Atlas Mountains	Morocco	11,500	2
Mt. Hood	Oregon	11,225	2
Mt. Lebanon	Syria	10,533	2
Mt. Perda, highest of Pyrenees	France	10,950	2
Mt. Ætna, volcano	Sicily	10,835	2
Monte Corno, highest of Apennines	Naples	9,523	1¾
Sneehattan, highest Dovrefield Mts	Norway	8,115	1½
Pindus, highest in	Greece	7,677	1½
Mount Sinai	Arabia	6,541	1¼
Black Mountain, highest in	N. Carolina	6,760	1¼
Mt. Washing, highest White Mts.	N. Hampshire	6,285	1¼
Mt. Marcy, highest in	New York	5,402	1
Mt. Hecla, volcano	Iceland	5,104	1
Ben Nevis, highest in Great Britain	Scotland	4,406	⅞
Mansfield, highest in Green Mts.	Vermont	4,280	¾
Peaks of Otter	Virginia	4,260	¾
Mt. Vesuvius	Naples	4,253	¾
Round Top, highest of Catskill Mts	New York	3,804	¾

Now and then we crossed spider-like bridges, looking so frail, that never again will I say anything against the stability of the Cornish viaducts. The only habitations one sees are a few log huts. My latin is a thing of the past, but the line "Facilis decensus averni" is very applicable to our descent, for we glided easily and rapidly to the plains below; but nothing, alas! in the shape of food was to be had. Soon the sun went down, leaving that soft, curious light we have so often mentioned—the snowy Rockies standing out in the foreground. As darkness came over us the driver tried to make up for the lost time, and about ten o'clock we thundered through the Royal Gorge of the Arkansas. The moon was very bright and well up in the heavens—we all stood on the tail-end of the Pullman (the last carriage) holding on like grim death—for the train swayed in an alarming manner as we were whisked round corners. The view was really grand—I may say awful—the Gorge very narrow, black, and lofty; the swollen river dashing over every obstacle and splashing the train with spray. In some places the chasm was so close that twenty feet would take in both torrent and line. Straight up above, some 700 to 1,200 feet, the black mountains glittered with feldspar, as every now and then the moon caught the crags. It was a *sensation* ride—for a lump of rock, a metal out of place, and nothing could have saved the train.

We turned in at eleven, having passed the worst place in the defile. As I write I can plainly see this wild pass so black and dreadful. I seemed to have hardly gone to sleep when the wretched black porter dug me in the ribs and said, "four o'clock; get up:" and, after a final struggle for a wash, L—— and I took our favourite stand on the back of the car, smoking and admiring the broad level sweep of rich green land. In the distance, our old friends, the Rockies. Upon reaching Denver, a charming little town of 58,000 inhabitants, we made for the Windsor Hotel—a large comfortable building, much larger and better than any hotel in Bristol—and the charges were fairly reasonable. Here we made a raid on the Turkish Bath, and enjoyed for the first time for a week the luxury of cleanliness. Denver has a superb Opera House—a fine brick building pointed with freestone. This house can take rank with any of the first London Theatres. This is a thriving and rapidly growing city. Here one sees no end of the "Rocky Mountain Elevator"—viz., the donkey in all shapes and sizes—he carries large burdens to the outlying districts. We left Denver, with some regret, at 9.25 p.m., and found the Pullman palace-cars of the Chicago, Burlington, and Quincy Railway—magnificent specimens of railway work—complete in every way, and two feet wider than those on the wretched Denver and Rio Grande. The distance to Chicago is 1052 miles—we performed the journey in absolute comfort—in fact, the railway journeys in the States are made with as much ease as it is possible to conceive; excepting, of course, the Rio Grande, and that cannot be too much condemned. The drivers of the engine of this horrid little line get as much as 37 dollars a-week, and that, with perquisites, is equal to £10 English money. The driver himself will tell you he does his best, but virtually carries accident in his hand. The track is frequently covered with rock or rubbish; and no true Government inspector should ever have passed as sound or safe such a villanous fraud.

To Chicago.

From Denver to Chicago everything went "merry as a marriage bell!" The Pullman palace-cars of the Chicago, Burlington, and Quincy Railway are really magnificent—the wood is of the finest, the cabinet and upholstery work is simply perfect—in fact, all over America, the carpenter, joiner, and cabinetmakers turn out good, solid, and tasteful effects, and with little of that hideous varnish so much in vogue in England. The interior of a Pullman palace-car is never disfigured by a single advertisement. The dining-car is quite distinct from the Pullman sleeping-car; and, as far as I could judge, would never, under any circumstances, be used as a sleeper. My first experience of a really good American dining-car was VERY pleasant, especially after our genuine discomfort on the Rio Grande. The dinner was perfect—even in New York I have taken worse meals. At the far end of the car the designer has placed the kitchen, carefully arranged, so that no smell of cooking should reach the passengers. The car has six small tables a-side, each table capable of holding four in comfort. The cooking all that could be desired, the waiting more than good, and the food various. Avoid wines, and stick to lager beer—

Milwaukee being, to my mind, the best—stick to it; leave claret, &c., &c., quite alone. I hope I may long remember my first dinner in an American dining-car—from a really capital menu we selected broiled fish, steak and mushrooms, vegetables, and finished with a strawberry ice. The waiter was a humorous black man, with a very large mouth, and marvellous set of teeth, muchly ornamented with gold—such ornamentation being evidently the work of a dental artist; his huge mouth and pug-dog eyes gave a laugh perfectly inimitable; his easy manner and skilful way of throwing up a plate and catching it again; his snow-white jacket, huge gold chain, stem-winder watch, large oblong stone ring, hair shaved to the skin, grand glossy complexion, and happy manner will long remain a memory. The napkins and table-linen simply spotless. The crafty little dodges for holding salt, pepper, sugar, &c., most ingenious —looking like tiny cabinets between the car windows. A large item in maintaining a sleeper-car is its washing bill; and from some paper I gathered the following figures:— The Pullman Coy.'s entire outfit includes 50,000 sheets, 46,000 pillow-slips, 13,000 blankets, 16,000 hand-towels, and 6,000 roller-towels. A car is entirely emptied and cleaned as soon as it reaches its destination; the linen is sent straight to the laundry; the number of table-cloths and napkins must, of course, be many more, *pro rata*. All I can say is this—everything is of the cleanest and best, the sheets are good, the blankets simply superb.

The average cost, per day and night, of a Pullman sleeper

is one dollar and a-half; or, say 6s. It is usual to give the nigger a quarter dollar each night, but don't, by any chance, offer the conductor a tip. The usual length of an American car is sixty feet—of course, worked on bogies. The car is one long room, with seats each side, and a passage down the centre—at one end, a lavatory and smoking-room, with iced water; at the other, ladies' toilet. The engines are strong and top-heavy looking, because of a huge black funnel, like an "overgrown wine-strainer;" in front a species of big gridiron—this is the cow-catcher. The railways being generally unenclosed, and the metals laid over farm-land, the cows have a chance of lying comfortably on the line; and frequently the engines, or rather locomotives, as they are called here, turns Mrs. Cow off rather suddenly. Not far from the funnel is a bell, which is rung often and at high pressure, when nearing or leaving a station. Many of the lines run straight through the streets of a town, so this precaution is useful. All the cars are of one class, but the almighty dollar provides the Pullman or palace-car, and

"That's the difference, sad to see,
 Betwixt my lord, the king, and me."

Never buy a limited ticket, if possible, but ask for a series of tickets that enable you to break your journey. Never travel in a "huckleberry train," *i.e.*, one that stops at all stations. Put your check-tickets in the band of your hat, and put your baggage-tickets in a pocket-book. This saves trouble. Men go round the train offering all sorts of things for sale—oranges, books, papers, bananas, &c. These men are rather a nuisance, but as a rule they are smart, and you may learn a new idea or so. The checking of baggage is one of the most delightful things in America. No matter how often you have to change trains with your hand-bag, which should contain just enough for the trip. The baggage itself is at the place you ordered it to be; you have a little brass-cheque given you with the number on one side, and a corresponding brass-label is fixed by a leather-loop to your baggage. When you arrive at (say Chicago), a parcel express man will gather your checks, learn the hotel, and give you a receipt for the baggage. This is all done for a very reasonable sum. Avoid letting your luggage remain long in a "depôt," for you have to pay so much a-day for each article.

Cunning little tables are set between the seats, and many a good game of cards has been enjoyed, although in our case the dust was a terrible nuisance. If you shut the window the heat was terrific; if we opened it the table was covered. Americans generally wear long white Holland ulsters,—these being of a glossy nature, somewhat counteract this nuisance. For a lady I should suggest a really good, fine alpaca ulster, with large hood. This would be useful in coaching or steamer, or by rail, and takes up little or no room. We lunched at Lincoln, Nebraska, and here the heat had been a day or so previously 109 in the shade. About three we struck the

Platte River, a tributary of the Missouri, a sluggish and very broad stream, suggestive of the Thames, and just now the Bristol Avon would hardly surpass it in colour. Shortly after we ran parallel with the Missouri itself (4,194 miles long)—here at least a mile wide, and banked with charming foliage. The land on either hand is under cultivation—corn, corn everywhere—everything most fertile in appearance.

The Longest and Greatest Rivers in the World.

RIVERS.	RISE.	DISCHARGE.	Miles.
Missouri	Rocky Mountains	Gulf of Mexico	4,194
Mississippi	Lake Itaska	Gulf of Mexico	2,616
Amazon	Andes	Atlantic Ocean	3,944
Hoang-Ho	Koulkoun Mountains	Yellow Sea	3,000
Murray	Australian Alps	Encounter Bay	3,000
Obi	Altaian Mountains	Arctic Ocean	2,800
Nile	Blue Nile, Abyssinia	Mediterranean	2,750
Yang-tse-Kia	Thibet	China Sea	2,500
Lena	Heights of Irkutsk	Arctic Ocean	2,500
Niger	Base of Mt. Loma	Gulf of Guinea	2,300
St. Lawrence	River St. Louis	Gulf of St. Lawrence	1,960
Volga	Lake in Volhonsky	Caspian Sea	1,900
Maykiang	Thibet	Chinese Gulf	1,700
Indus	Little Thibet	Arabian Sea	1,700
Danube	Black Forest	Black Sea	1,630
Mackenzie	River Athabasco	Arctic Ocean	2,500
Brahmapootra	Himalaya	Bay of Bengal	1,500
Columbia	Rocky Mountains	Pacific Ocean	1,090
Colorado	San Iaba	Gulf of California	1,000
Susquehanna	Lake Otsego	Chesapeake Bay	400
James	Alleghany Mountains	Chesapeake Bay	500
Potomac	Gr. Black Bone Mts.	Chesapeake Bay,	400
Hudson	Adirond'ks, Mt. Marcy	Bay of New York	325

At last we reached "Wonderful Chicago," and, although there happened to be a meeting of Delegates to select or nominate the new President, we got good rooms at the Palmer House—another mighty Hotel. I can safely say the hall was hardly safe to walk upon, for it had been used as one huge spittoon, and everywhere the free and enlightened voter had left traces of his salivary industry—the Yankee crest should be a Spittoon Rampant. The Palmer House is a fine Hotel, and with far better feeding than the Palace, and everything nicer and cheaper. The Sunday dinner was simply perfection. The enclosed Menu will give you some idea of what we had to select from:—

THE "PALMER."

DINNER.

Little Neck Clams on Shell.

Anglaise Soup.

Halibut au Gratin.

Boiled Leg of Mutton, Caper Sauce;
Corned Beef and Cabbage;
Sugar-cured Ham.

Roast Beef;
Spring Lamb, Mint Sauce;
Turkey, Giblet Sauce.

Calf's Head en Tortue;
Sweetbreads, with Puree of Spinach;
Small Patties au Salbiquon;
Lamb Chops Breaded au Jus;
Fried Frogs a la Crapotine.

Smoked Beef Tongue;
Chicken Salad;   Spiced Oysters;
Salmon a la Mayonaise.

Cucumbers;   Sliced Tomatoes;
Currant Jelly.

Mashed Potatoes;   Cabbage;
Boiled Potatoes;   Stewed Tomatoes;
Stewed Onions;   Sweet Corn;
Asparagus.

Steamed Fruit Pudding, Cognac Sauce;
Cherry Pie;   Cocoanut Meringue Pie;
Imperial Wine Jelly;   Assorted Cake;
Macaroons;   Confectionery;
Ice Cream a la Nesselrode;   Siberian Punch.

Claret;   Sweet Cider.

Mixed Nuts;   Fruit;   Raisins;
Edam, Roquefort, and American Cheese.

Coffee;
Water Melon.

Chicago is the capital of Illinois and Western America, and now numbers 640,000 inhabitants, and less than fifty years ago a hundred souls could not have been found. Most of us can recall the terrible fires of 1871 and 1874 that overtook this young city, but now no trace of their havoc remains, and the marvellous growth of Chicago is without a parallel in the history of modern times. It is situated on Lake Michigan, and has a climate similar to that of Paris, and a breeze comes off the Lake by day, and changes to nearly an exact opposite at night. This grand city covers an area of fifty square miles, and is as level as a garden—the whole laid out in square blocks—but the authorities have kept some large, well-laid out parks for the public benefit, and Lincoln Park is a fine sample of what a public park should be.

I could write about Chicago for hours, and then never give you half a notion of its go-aheadedness. The electric light is used everywhere possible, and the street wire-trams are fast and easy travelling. I should not lay myself open to contradiction if I said Chicago is the most wonderful city in the world. The Union Stockyards are unrivalled for size, and some of the curing establishments are huge systems of reducing Mr. Pig to bacon, sausages, &c., impossible to describe. The butcher can kill with ease 500 per hour in a most artistic manner, and a few minutes after the sides, &c., are in the freezing room. Ask for street car, Thirty-Ninth Street, and then take tram to Union Stockyards, and get permission to see over Mr. Fowler's. He employs 3,000 men. There are two parallel continuous streets in Chicago fourteen miles in length, and with houses numbered to over 3,000. The Fire Department is the most thoroughly equipped in the world. The men are fine-looking, well-dressed, and understand their business thoroughly. The horses are large, well-built, intelligent creatures, and as alert to their duty as the men.

Size of Lakes, Seas, and Oceans.

LAKE.	Miles Long.	Miles Wide.	SEAS.	Miles Long.
Superior	380	120	Mediterranean	2,000
Michigan	330	60	Caribbean	1,800
Ontario	180	40	China	1,700
Champlain	123	12	Red	1,400
Erie	270	50	Japan	1,000
Huron	250	90	Black	932
Cayuga	36	4	Caspian	640
George	36	3	Baltic	600
Baikal	360	35	Okhotsk	600
Great Slave	300	45	White	450
Winnipeg	240	40	Aral	250
Athabasco	200	20		
Maracaybo	150	60	OCEANS.	Miles Square.
Great Bear	150	40	Pacific	80,000,000
Ladoga	125	75	Atlantic	40,000,000
Constance	45	10	Indian	20,000,000
Geneva	50	10	Southern	10,000,000
Lake of the Woods	70	25	Arctic	5,000,000

NIAGARA, &c.

We left Chicago on Sunday afternoon per 4.15 train of the Michigan Central for Niagara, and arrived at the Clifton House Hotel, Canadian side, at nine next morning. I will say nothing about these grand set of falls, for thousands have written of their beauty and the terrible impositions imposed upon the unfortunate "globe trotter;" and I can only hope the time may come when this beautiful place will have every house, except two or three ornamental and useful hotels, removed at least a mile from the river-bed, and when the red Virginia creeper will be allowed to grow up the side of the cliffs and stand out in rich contrast to pine-shaded slopes and the bright creamy green water. Take a carriage by the day, eight dollars all told, and share this between four; take bridge tickets from the hotel, do the Canadian side Whirlpool, Prospect Place, Goat Island, &c., before lunch. After lunch take a drive to Fire Spring, &c., and then quietly back to dinner. Don't have your photograph taken, and don't buy all the rubbish you see. Sunday is rather a good day at Niagara, for the " tout pest " is generally eased off, and the hawkers, guides, photograph-mongers are fewer. The girls in the shops pounce upon you and nearly insist upon your buying something. The Indian curios are mostly quite a fraud, and probably made in Buffalo or New York.

From Niagara we took train and steamer to Toronto on Lake Ontario. The Queen's is a good and comfortable hotel. Book your berth on board the next day's steamer at once. See a trotting-match, if possible. The steam trip to Montreal down the Thousand Islands is very beautiful, and the Lachine Rapids are worth doing, but are hardly as exciting as tourists generally make out. We steamed under the Grand Victoria Tubular Bridge at six o'clock, and half-an-hour after saw us in the Windsor Hotel, Montreal, one of the best hotels in the world, and by no means expensive. A week in Montreal is none too much, and during our stay the weather was bracing and fresh. We started by the early morning train for Lake Champlain, and thence through Lake George to Fort-William, where we took the stage-coach to Saratoga.

SARATOGA.

I have been to a great many places in my life, and seen every variety of town, but the life at a Saratoga hotel baffles all my powers of description. The town itself is nothing, but the hotels are simply huge caravansaries, and during my stay crammed with the *elite* of American society, our two selves being the only Britishers there. From what I could gather, sixty days are regarded by the hotel-keepers as constituting a season of the ordinary length, and there would never be any grumbling if good weather and average receipts began with the 1st July and ended 1st September. These hotels keep up an immense force of employees, incurring a large daily expenditure. In the height of the season, when all is rush, jostle, and push, the United States Hotel accommodates nightly an average of 1,000 to 1,200 guests, and the Grand Union about the same number. The item of service is one of the most serious a great hotel encounters. 50,000 dollars was what the United States Hotel paid for help in one season alone. Some people, doubtless, imagine the manager of a large hotel has little else to do beside lolling in his private office, sucking cobbler through a straw, or smoking a cigar. Such, I can safely imagine, is far from the fact; and I should fancy the man at the other end of the straw must be often fagged and weary. To enforce the necessary system for carrying on such a big thing, must have constant attention. The housekeeper has her squads of chambermaids directed on each floor by a chief assistant. The head waiter has his deputies, who divide up the dining-room between them. I feel sure in the laundry a more than usually well-ordered system has to be followed, else there would be confusion worse than the laundry girls must have made in Babel's time. 965 dined in the one large hall the day I made my inquiries, and say one-third were men; I can positively affirm that the black man in the vestibule—the receiver of hats, caps, gloves, sticks, &c.—took from these 300 men one, and sometimes all, of the above-named articles, and with neither ticket nor pigeon-holes he returned each man's property without a blunder, or the slightest hesitation—this is purely an effort of memory.

Mount MacGregor is an object of interest, lying about 1,000 feet above Saratoga Springs. From its summit you can see the dim outline of Adirondacks, the Green Mountain range, and in the hazy distance the Catskills. Lakes, patches of forest, and farm lands, stretch as far as the eye can reach. We had very little time to spare at Saratoga, so I tried a glass of each kind of water in the one afternoon, and I fancy one must have neutralised the others, for I never heard any more about them.

The hotels are constructed round an immense quadrangle, the inside square being a large garden planted with forest trees, and beautifully laid out with band-stand in centre and shady nooks in every imaginable place. The dining, drawing, smoking, and ball-rooms are on the ground floor, and open out into a broad-covered verandah—the verandah itself forming a jolly chatting or walking place. It was very hot here during our stay—the silver fluid in the glass tube palpitated, expanded, and gradually climbed its way up and up until it reached the nineties; even here it did not stop, but still upward, and at three o'clock 95° was touched. The dancing here is good, also the music. I was introduced to about 400 colonels and at least 40 judges. I fancy the former must be manufactured on the spot. I was also introduced by the M.C. to a very nice little American. She told me her father was an oyster merchant, and I knew all about her brothers and sisters, cousins, aunts, in less than ten minutes. After two dances she said, "Come along, we will go and see Uncle John in the Grand Union." We started off down the street of Saratoga—she in her ball-dress, I in my war-paint, both without hat or bonnet; and soon we were taking drinks with Uncle John, and dancing to the strain of a fresh band in the ball-room of the Grand Union. Picnics, laughing, chatting, flirting, and dancing, to say nothing of smoking, form the principal attractions of Saratoga. We left by the eleven o'clock night mail for New York, and reached that city early next morning.

New York and Brooklyn Bridge.

First talked of by Colonel Julius W. Adams about 1855. Act of incorporation passed April, 1866. Survey begun by John A. Roebling, 1869. Construction begun January 2, 1870. First rope thrown across the river, August 14, 1876. Master Mechanic Farrington crossed in a boatswain's chair, August 25, 1876. Depth of the New York foundation below high-water mark, 78 feet 6 inches. Depth of the Brooklyn foundation below high-water mark, 45 feet. The New York tower contains 46,945 cubic yards of masonry; the Brooklyn tower, 38,214. Weight of the Brooklyn tower, about 93,079 tons. Weight of the New York tower, about a third more. Size of the towers at high-water line 140 × 59 feet; at roof-course, 136 × 53 feet. Height of the towers above high-water mark, 276 feet 6 inches. Height of roadway in the clear in the middle of the East River, 135 feet. Grade of the roadway, 3 feet 3 inches to 100 feet. Width of the promenade in the centre of bridge, 16 feet 7 inches. Width for railway on one side of the promenade, 12 feet 10 inches. Width of carriage way on the other side of the promenade, 18 feet 9 inches. Width of bridge, 85 feet. Length of main span, 1,595 feet 6 inches. Length of each land span, 930 feet. Length of the Brooklyn approach, 971 feet. Length of the New York approach, 1,560 feet. Length of each of the four great cables, 3,578 feet 6 inches; diameter, 15¾ inches; number of steel-galvanised wires in each cable, 5,434; weight of each cable, about 800 tons. Ultimate strength of each cable, 15,000 tons. Weight of steel in the suspended superstructure, 10,000 tons. Total cost, 15,000,000 dollars. Opened for traffic in 1883.

We put up at the celebrated Fifth Avenue Hotel, and paid six dollars a day for room and food; but my advice to say a couple or three men travelling together would be, take a dollar and a-half or two-dollar bed-room each at the Brunswick; breakfast, lunch, and dine where you like—not forgetting that one portion at a restaurant is often enough for three—always more than sufficient for two.

New York is so familiar to us all now, and so near, by means of our floating hotels, that I will say nothing about it. If you want a really good English chop, or a dozen Blue Point oysters, go to John Ronan, 503 Broadway. Walk once from top to bottom of Broadway. Call in and see Tiffineys, the large jeweller. Always use the Elevated Way when you can. Spend a night or so at the Casino Theatre, and have supper on the roof. Attend service at St. Thomas' Church, Fifth Avenue. Do Manhattan and Coney Island. Go to Greenwood Cemetery. Go up the Hudson to Albany. Take the Fall River Line and steamer *Pilgrim* for Boston, and stay when there at the Hotel Vendome.

I have seen a good deal of Americans now, having twice visited the great Continent, and for twelve years I was thrown against them—very often at the Langham Hotel in London—and I can pass an opinion founded on some observation. That the bulk are boastful and bad-mannered is unquestioned (I am only talking of the bulk), but the really educated American is very nice indeed, full of dry humour, with broad views, able and willing to give information, and unbounded in hospitality. The real Religion of the Americans is Dollarology. He worships the Dollar. Of course, a man must be sufficiently crafty to make his dollars in such a way that he is not within the pale of the law, but it is of very little moment to the average American who sinks as long as he swims. The typical American likes show, the insignia being a huge oblong finger-ring for the men, and diamonds in daylight for the women. They have a leaning for 'cuteness rather than honesty. Their statesmen are smart, very smart, and push along at a grand pace—the shrewdest people in the world—but I fear all this smartness has a tendency to lessen in the sight of the rising · generation the value of honesty and truth, and any one resisting the temptation to make money in a questionable speculation would be regarded with ridicule rather than respect. Anyway, from what I have heard, read, and seen of the American Stock Exchange, and especially the New York branch of that powerful body, I can safely say this, that Americans themselves feel very little confidence in their dealings, and the whole body are generally under a cloud of suspicion. There must be in every country rising and falling markets, but in America there is no real steadiness, and if a rise in the price of securities occurs, the public mind is possessed by the not unnatural suspicion that the advance has been caused by the manipulation of some clique of speculators interested in getting rid of heavier burdens than they like to carry. Indeed, as far as I could see, the worst characteristic of the New York Stock Market is the common lack of confidence in the integrity of those who control it. When men of enormous wealth—all of which must be subject to decrease or increase by the operations of Wall Street—combine to protect themselves, the public must stand aloof or be crushed. I shall never forget the Petroleum Stock Room, and as we wended our way back to the Brunswick my mind was filled with the fascination of being rich in a hurry. I think I better understood on that day what the word gambler meant. It is the great available wealth of these men, and their disposition to use it without being too particular about the manner of using it, which has served in such a great degree to impair public confidence in the American Stock Exchange. These wire-pullers will let their friends in in their efforts to secure themselves. The J—— G—— of America are the ruin of all honest stock-broking; the public are at the mercy of such men, and the public are now beginning to know that mercy is a quality quite out of the question, and are avoiding the markets in which these men play their tricks—the Jack and trout don't live well together. There is no other country on the face of the earth where money counts for so much as it does in this country. "There is no other country in the world where it excuses so many mean and dirty dealings in the making of this money, and there is no country in the world where it is so recklessly, unwisely, or vulgarly spent, or where it returns so little to the spender." The simple life of industry is being hitched up together with that of the gambler. High and low, rich and poor, are gradually becoming gamblers, and men who, like G—— G——, held a high reputation, are induced to carry that reputation to the market and sell the lot for what it may fetch.

The Americans as a body are vulgar, for they have not arrived at the threshold of finding out that tawdry display is not happiness, and that simple industry, plain living, and self-denial are higher attributes for a young and glorious country to aim at than that feverish haste to be rich at no matter what cost. Who shall say where this lively taste for vulgarities, extravagances, and exaggerations will lead this marvellous nation?

Let money be at stake, and all over the world you will see human nature with the paint off.

The Americans seem to have imbibed into their veins the restless haste and hunger to rise, which is the source of much that is good and most that is evil in the life of this fine people. I'm hot; 92° in the shade, so enough for the day!!

There is one thing that will strike you about New York: no bright window-boxes in the houses, no pretty beds or borders in the splendid Central Park, and the suburbs nothing but long straight lines of warm red stone. A cab or carriage drive in New York is a luxury, and should not be indulged in without some consideration. I paid for an afternoon drive of two hours and a half the sum of eight dollars, or 32s. I must admit the carriage, man, and horses were very good, but it taught caution.

I agree with the *Standard* that there is no place in the world where cooling drinks are better understood than in America. With the thermometer from 90° to 97°, the claims of even pleasure or business are for the time put aside for the more temporarily important subject of iced drinks. The natural evaporation during this excessive heat makes renewal a pleasing necessity. The names of Brother Jonathan's drinks are legion—mint julep, egg nob, John Collins, soda-lemonade, corpse reviver, whisky, gin, and brandy cock-tails, *ad infinitum*. No bars in the world are more tempting or better served than those across the Atlantic. The Hoffman House, Fifth Avenue, New York, is worthy a visit, if only from an artistic point of view. "Iced goat" is, I believe, the latest drink. The bar-tender must have the knowledge of a Mephistopheles and the manipulation of Herr Dobler, this white-jacketed, clean-shaven man has everything at hand. To say that these drinks are inexpensive is an error, for twenty cents, or 10d., is about the usual price for nearly all short drinks, but the quantity of ice used and wasted in the preparation of your drink must be taken into consideration. My advice to a stranger in New York during the summer months is moderation in iced drinks, for I feel sure half the dyspepsia in the States and the great demand for and success of American dentists, is due to ice. Iced water at breakfast, iced water at dinner, iced water at night—in fact, ice in every available way. I must admit that an old tom cock-tail, followed by a tumbler of water with tiny icebergs peeping above the surface is very nice, but I say again, avoid this cold enchantress. If you want a simple glass of spirit ask for whisky straight or brandy straight, and you will have the bottle handed to you so that you may help yourself. The most poetic of the American drinks, as far as names go, are "bosom caresser" and "fairy kisses." The American language is very graphic, and the following instance struck me as being very good :—If they can't float a public company as easily as was at first supposed, they will tell you that "coach has stopped for repairs."

As far as I could judge, the members of their legislative body are simply delegates, not representatives, of one or other political party, consequently at the beck and call of the political wire-pullers.

The Produce Exchange, New York, is a very fine, complete, and useful building, saving labour, and concentrating the corn and produce business. The view of New York from the Tower is the finest to be obtained. 20,000 people danced in this enormous building the day it was opened. Personally, I very much admire the solid architecture, well-arranged offices, and smart lifts. Having taken our passage on board the *Oregon*, now owned by the Cunard Co., and finding I had a day or so to spare, M—— and I ran up by the Fall River Line to Boston; and I think a slight description of the steamer *Pilgrim* will give you some idea of what Yankees can and will do. Always take your *berth* and tickets two or three days before, to avoid sleeping on a mattress in the saloon. The following description is mostly taken from the Company's foot-notes, but nothing is beyond the fact; for photographs or illustrations can but in a very inadequate manner convey a correct impression of this really great and beautiful marine mammoth, which is controlled as easily as a small tug-boat.

Principal dimensions—Length on deck 390 feet, beam of the hull proper 50 feet, beam over guards 87 feet 6 inches, depth of hold 18 feet 6 inches, depth from upper deck to hold 60 feet, tonnage 3,500 registered tons—making her by far the largest inland steamer in the world. Her motive power consists of a vertical beam-engine, with a cylinder of 110 inches in diameter, stroke of piston 14 feet, working under a maximum steam-pressure of 50 pounds to the square inch. She has twelve boilers made of steel, developing in all 5,500 horse-power. She is a ship within a ship, and has 103 water-tight compartments. 25 feet from her stern is the water-tight collision bulk-head, 50 feet abaft the stern is another bulk-head. The *Pilgrim* has her engines and boilers enclosed in iron bulk-heads, rendering it impossible for fire from boilers or kitchen to reach any other part of the boat. The introduction of electricity has reduced the chances of fire to the most infinitesimal points, there being no fire in any part of the vessel, except in this same boiler-room and kitchen. The electric plant on the *Pilgrim* is Edison's, and consists of 912 lamps—1 L and 2 K dynamos, with a capacity of 11,382 candle power, and worked by two engines. Care has been taken, throughout the whole wiring, to provide such a system as to prevent the lights from being extinguished by any accident to the boat; and so the wiring has been divided into four independent sections. You can go into your berth, and at any moment turn on and turn off this beautiful light. The grand saloon is illuminated by one magnificent electrolier of 36 lights, and two smaller electroliers of 27 lights each. The light in State-Room continues all night. I hardly know where to begin in the description of the *Pilgrim*, but will imagine we are entering this huge ship from the wharf on her starboard side (right-hand side, facing bows). The *Pilgrim* can never have a jammed gangway, for the purser's room is on the port side. The lavatory is a huge place, in which the barber has comfortable quarters; and, talking about barbers, there are none better, or more expensive, than the artist barbers of America.

The grand saloon is now the point to which we turn our steps, having taken our state-room and tickets days before. This is the largest and finest steamboat saloon in the world, being 320 feet in length. Its dome roof is 20 feet 6 inches from the deck, and is 280 feet long. This grand saloon will hold 1,400 passengers comfortably. The ceiling overhead and under the gallery is frescoed in party-colours, giving a most charming effect. In this grand saloon are 103 state-rooms, seven bridal chambers, and two family bridals. The bridal rooms have two folding bedsteads, so that the room is in fact a drawing-room until the time of retiring. These rooms have ceilings frescoed with cupids, sea-nymphs, and urchins. The ordinary state-rooms are models of comfort with spring beds, the best of hair mattresses, feather pillows, and spotless bed linen, lace and damask curtains. Only in selecting a state-room, don't forget to get as far away from the paddle-wheels as possible. The dining-hall has sixteen tables capable of seating at one time 170 persons. Forward of this are the servants' quarters, where 54 men are berthed nightly. The huge proportions of this ship are softened by her symmetry, and really the whole bulk looks small. She cost one million sterling, and is a floating monument to the skill, enterprise, ability, and scientific attainments of the American engineer and mechanic. The night I was on board over 1,400 passengers were comfortably provided for.

HOMEWARD BOUND.

Trevithick came down to see us off. We started early on the morning of the 26th June. The *Oregon* is a grand specimen of what the English shipbuilder can do, her speed averaging about 420 knots. But I am now becoming bankrupt in adjectives, so I will not try to describe her. The huge saloon, in plain white and gold, affords a pretty contrast to the coloured glass swinging in the racks above. This ship moves very steadily; but no matter how hot it may be in New York, nor how tempting the sun, don't fail to put on thick underclothing, for the speed causes a great falling of the temperature, and congestion of the liver may be the result.

Directly you get on board order your bath at a given time, and at once select your seat at table. We arrived at Queenstown in 6 days 14 hours and 1 minute, very nearly the fastest time on record. It was a glorious day, sea calm as a mirror, as we steamed past Anglesea, making a slight dip into Carnarvon Bay, with the dotted houses of Llandudno in the distance. During the voyage the beating the *America* (who up to the present had done the fastest time on record) was all the theme; and we only lost by a quarter of an hour. We both sent up a British cheer as the rivals passed each other just outside the Liverpool bar, she on her way across the Herring Pond and Westward Ho!

The Custom House at Liverpool is the worst in the world. The cramming and jamming is enough to make the American sneer at our want of system. What can you expect when I tell you that these officials get paid £65 per annum, and have to work for ninety hours per week; they must always appear respectable, and even the Sabbath is not their own. We left all baggage in the shed, drove to the hotel, washed and dined, and returned at ten for our luggage, where we still found many of our fellow-passengers struggling with their boxes, &c. We soon got our lot passed, and in less than half an hour were smoking a quiet pipe at the London and North-Western Hotel, having done some 30,000 miles at a cost of £450 each at the outside, having seen, during the eight months, many of the landscape wonders of the world.

Fictitious Names of States.

BADGER STATE.—A name popularly given to the State of Wisconsin.

BAY STATE.—A popular name of Massachusetts, which, previous to the adoption of the Federal Constitution, was called the Colony of Massachusetts Bay.

BAYOU STATE.—A name sometimes given to the State of Mississippi, which abounds in bayous, or creeks.

BEAR STATE.—A name by which the State of Arkansas is sometimes designated, on account of the number of bears that formerly infested its forests.

CREOLE STATE.—A name sometimes given to the State of Louisiana, in which the descendants of the original French and Spanish settlers constitute a large proportion of the population.

DIAMOND STATE.—A name sometimes given to the State of Delaware, from its small size and great worth, or supposed importance.

EMPIRE STATE.—A popular name of the State of New York, the most populous and the wealthiest State in the Union.

EXCELSIOR STATE.—The State of New York, sometimes so called from the motto "Excelsior" upon its coat of arms.

FREESTONE STATE.—The State of Connecticut, sometimes so called from the quarries of freestone which it contains.

GRANITE STATE.—A popular name for the State of New Hampshire, the mountainous portions of which are largely composed of granite.

GREEN MOUNTAIN STATE.—A popular name for the State of Vermont, the Green Mountains being the principal mountain range in the State.

HAWKEYE STATE.—The State of Iowa, said to be so named after an Indian Chief, who was once a terror to VOYAGEURS to its borders.

HOOSIER STATE.—The State of Indiana, the inhabitants of which are often called HOOSIERS. This word is a corruption of HUSHER, formerly a common term for a bully throughout the West.

KEYSTONE STATE.—The State of Pennsylvania, so called from its having been the central State of the Union at the time of the formation of the Constitution. If the names of the thirteen original States are arranged in the form of an arch, Pennsylvania will occupy the place of the keystone.

LAKE STATE.—A name popularly given to the State of Michigan, which borders upon the four lakes—Superior, Michigan, Huron, and Erie.

LONE-STAR STATE.—The State of Texas, so called from the device on its coat of arms.

LUMBER STATE.—A popular designation for the State of Maine, the inhabitants of which are largely engaged in the business of cutting and rafting lumber, or of converting it into boards, shingles, scantlings, and the like.

MOTHER OF PRESIDENTS.—A name frequently given in the United States to the State of Virginia, which has furnished six presidents to the Union.

MOTHER OF STATES.—A name sometimes given to Virginia, the first settled of the thirteen States which united in the Declaration of Independence.

NUTMEG STATE.—A popular name, in America, for the State of Connecticut, the inhabitants of which have such a reputation for shrewdness, that they have been jocosely accused of palming off wooden nutmegs on unsuspecting purchasers, instead of the genuine article.

OLD COLONY.—A name popularly given to that portion of Massachusetts included within the original limits of the Plymouth colony, which was formed at an earlier date than the colony of Massachusetts Bay.

OLD DOMINION.—A popular name for the State of Virginia.

OLD NORTH STATE.—A popular designation of the State of North Carolina.

PALMETTO STATE.—The State of South Carolina, so called from the arms of the State, which contain a palmetto.

PENINSULAR STATE.—The State of Florida, so called from its shape.

PINE-TREE STATE.—A popular name of the State of Maine, the central and northern portions of which are covered with extensive pine forests.

PRAIRIE STATE.—A name given to Illinois in allusion to the widespread and beautiful prairies, which form a striking feature of the scenery of the State.

TURPENTINE STATE.—A popular name for the State of North Carolina, which produces and exports immense quantities of turpentine.

Fictitious Names of Cities.

BLUFF CITY.—A descriptive name popularly given to the city of Hannibal, Missouri.

CITY OF BROTHERLY LOVE.—Philadelphia is sometimes so called, this being the literal signification of the name.

CITY OF CHURCHES.—A name popularly given to the city of Brooklyn, N.Y., from the unusually large number of churches which it contains.

CITY OF ELMS.—A familiar denomination of New Haven, Conn., many of the streets of which are thickly shaded with lofty elms.

CITY OF MAGNIFICENT DISTANCES.—A popular designation given to the city of Washington, the capital of the United States, which is laid out on a very large scale, being intended to cover a space four miles and a half long, and two miles and a half broad, or eleven square miles. The entire site is traversed by two sets of streets, from 70 to 100 feet wide, at right angles to one another, the whole again intersected obliquely by fifteen avenues from 130 to 160 feet wide.

CITY OF NOTIONS.—In the united States, a popular name for the city of Boston, Mass., the metropolis of Yankeedom.

CITY OF ROCKS.—A descriptive name popularly given, in the United States, to the city of Nashville, Tenn.

CITY OF SPINDLES.—A name popularly given to the city of Lowell, Mass., the largest cotton-manufacturing town in the United States.

CITY OF THE STRAITS.—A name popularly given to Detroit which is situated on the west bank of the river or strait connecting Lake St. Clair with Lake Erie. DETROIT is a French word meaning "strait."

CRESCENT CITY.—A popular name for the city of New Orleans, the older portion of which is built around the convex side of a bend of the Mississippi River.

EMPIRE CITY.—The city of New York, the chief city of the western world, and the metropolis of the Empire State.

FALL CITY.—Louisville, Ky., popularly so called from the falls which, at this place, impede the navigation of the Ohio River.

FLOUR CITY.—A popular designation, in the United States, for the city of Rochester, N.Y., a place remarkable for its extensive manufactories of flour.

FLOWER CITY.—Springfield, Illinois, the capital of the state, which is distinguished for the beauty of its surroundings.

FOREST CITY.—1. Cleveland, Ohio, so called from the many ornamental trees with which the streets are bordered.

2. A name given to Portland, Maine, a city distinguished for its many elms and other beautiful shade trees.

GARDEN CITY.—A popular name for Chicago, a city which is remarkable for the number and beauty of its private gardens.

GARDEN OF THE WEST.—A name usually given to Kansas, but sometimes applied to Illinois and others of the Western States which are all noted for their high productiveness.

GATE CITY.—Keokuk, Iowa, popularly so called. It is situated at the foot of the lower rapids of the Mississippi.

GOTHAM.—A popular name for the city of New York.

HUB OF THE UNIVERSE.—A burlesque and popular designation of Boston, Mass., originating with the American humourist, O. W. Holmes.

IRON CITY.—A name popularly given in the United States to

Pittsburg, Pa., a city distinguished for its numerous and immense iron manufactures.

MONUMENTAL CITY.—The city of Baltimore, so called from the monuments which it contains.

MOUND CITY.—A name popularly given to St. Louis, on account of the numerous artificial mounds that occupied the site on which the city is built.

PURITAN CITY.—A name sometimes given to the city of Boston, Mass., in allusion to the character of its founders and early inhabitants.

QUAKER CITY.—A popular name of Philadelphia, which was planned and settled by William Penn.

QUEEN CITY.—A popular name of Cincinnati, so called when it was the undisputed commercial metropolis of the West.

QUEEN CITY OF THE LAKES.—A name sometimes given to the city of Buffalo, N.Y., from its position and importance.

RAILROAD CITY.—Indianapolis, the capital of the State of Indiana, is sometimes called by this name, as being the terminus of various railroads.

SMOKY CITY.—A name sometimes given to Pittsburg, an important manufacturing city of Pennsylvania.

www.ingramcontent.com/pod-product-compliance
Lightning Source LLC
Chambersburg PA
CBHW020240170426
43202CB00008B/164